THE MONEY MONARCHS

The Secrets of 10 of America's
Best Investment Managers

THE MONEY MONARCHS
The Secrets of 10 of America's Best Investment Managers

Douglas J. Donnelly

IRWIN
Professional Publishing
Burr Ridge, Illinois
New York, New York

Senior editor:	Amy Hollands Gaber
Project editor:	Paula M. Buschman
Production manager:	Bob Lange
Cover designer:	Tim Kaage
Art coordinator:	Heather Burbridge
Art studio:	Jay Benson Studios
Compositor:	TCSystems, Inc.
Typeface:	11/13 Palatino
Printer:	Book Press

Library of Congress Cataloging-in-Publication Data

Donnelly, Douglas J.
  The money monarchs : the secrets of 10 of America's best
investment managers / by Douglas J. Donnelly.
      p.   cm.
    ISBN 1-55623-898-3
    1. Investment advisors—United States. 2. Investments—United
States. I. Title.
HG4928.5.D66 1994
332.6—dc20   93–16648

Printed in the United States of America
  3 4 5 6 7 8 9 0 BP 0 9 8 7 6 5 4 3

Dedication

To my wife, Jeri, who gave me unwavering support and shouldered the burden of taking care of three supercharged little boys (Connor, Ross, and Patrick, ages three through seven) while I was busy managing my clients' portfolios during the day or holed up in my office writing at night and on weekends. As my father always reminds me, "How did a guy from Longview, Washington, ever get so lucky?"

Message to the Reader—Why I Wrote this Book

"The things which hurt, instruct"

Benjamin Franklin

As a portfolio and financial adviser, I have made a wide range of investment decisions over the years with my clients as well as my personal accounts. Some of these investments have been extremely profitable. Unfortunately, some have lost money. And although generating a large capital gain for a client is always an exciting and rewarding experience, realizing the loss of a large chunk of capital in an unprofitable investment is an unforgettably painful feeling. These investment experiments—both good and bad—have left permanent imprints on my mind.

I, like most investors, have chased the newest hot investment strategy. From time to time, I believed that I had found the secret to hitting that elusive financial home run. Unfortunately, I also found that, as in baseball, those batters who hit the most home runs are often those who lead the league in strikeouts.

I wrote this book to reduce your probability of striking out.

This is not a "how to" investment book about the latest (and bogus) investment strategy or beating the market with no risk. Rather, this is an in-depth review of 10 of America's most successful money managers and their investment philosophies, strategies, and portfolio disciplines.

Do these top-ranked advisers make mistakes? Every day! In fact, in writing this book I run the risk of turning you, the reader, into a guru groupie or worshipper, someone who makes the incorrect assumption that these investment advisers can do no wrong. These 10 advisers are not clairvoyant. During market downturns, 70 to 80 percent of all stocks will decline—even if your adviser is a great stock picker!

Practical and real-life equity-oriented (stock) strategies are detailed and reviewed. For those of you scared to death of any risk and who prefer to keep your money under the mattress or in a checking account, I suggest you not change your philosophy. But for those of you who want to stay ahead of inflation and generate capital gains, this book will prove to be invaluable.

Each manager highlighted takes risks on a daily basis, but does so in a controlled manner. Because the managers adhere to their disciplines, client portfolios have survived and prospered over complete, long-term business cycles.

The 10 managers have met strict performance criteria which place them at the top of my list of outstanding money managers. Basically, they have consistently generated above-average returns for their clients with lower risk. And that's good enough for me and my clients!

Preface

This book will assist investors, retirement plan sponsors, brokers, financial planners, and investment advisers to:

- Develop their own accurate and tailored investment profile/personality.
- Match this personality to a top-ranked money manager.
- Monitor and evaluate their money manager(s).
- Understand how some of America's top-ranked managers think, manage portfolios, and control risk.
- Make a few dollars in profit!

Additionally, it covers the issues associated with wrap-fee programs, in which the client and the broker are, for once, on the same side of the table. Although the use of money managers is the fastest growing business on Wall Street, little literature has been written on the subject. Additionally, what the reader will find interesting and helpful is that although each manager has completely different and seemingly opposite investment philosophies and strategies, over the long term, each of their performances is within a few percentage points of the others. In other words, here are 10 managers who have their own unique ways of "skinning the cat."

I have learned a tremendous amount from these people, both about life and portfolio investment strategy. I hope the reader will capture the same benefits.

Douglas J. Donnelly

Acknowledgments

I want to thank these people who made the completion of this book project possible:

To Kathy Keller, my local editor and friend, who reviewed and revised all the chapters and whose valuable input vastly improved the final version. Had she not agreed to help me, I am not sure I would have initiated the project.

To Ricardo Cortez, who would have been the coauthor had he not been promoted to New York. His work in the inception stages got the project off the ground, especially in developing the concepts for the introduction and setting up the initial interviews.

To Kathy Leszcynski, who faithfully and without *any* complaints waded through my poor handwriting and continuous script modifications to type all the chapters.

To Amy Hollands and Ralph Rieves at Business One Irwin, who not only accepted the project, but gave me the needed free rein.

To all my clients, who have entrusted me with the management of their portfolios through both good and bad economic periods. Put bluntly, without my clients my portfolio manager position would not exist. I never forget where my bread is buttered.

To Paul Wonnacott, Jerry Bosch, Fred Weiss, Ross Kusian, Frank Alibimi, Halvaard Kvaale, Erland Bo, Rick Roeder, and Darren Decupero, who provided technical and administrative support.

To all the managers I interviewed for the book, who so graciously gave me their organizations' and personal time.

And finally and most importantly, to my family, who instilled in me the confidence and work ethic to take on and complete a project of this nature and scope.

D. J. D.

Table of Contents

Chapter Twelve
SYSTEMATIC FINANCIAL MANAGEMENT, INC. RETURN OF THE ACCOUNTING NERDS   178

Chapter Thirteen
SUMMARY WHAT WE CAN LEARN FROM THESE PROS   194

Chapter One

Introduction to Portfolio Management

"If you don't know who you are, the stock market is an expensive place to find out."

Adam Smith (George J.W. Goodman, *The Money Game*)

Today's investor is both blessed and confused by the wide spectrum of investment choices available. While the barriers to professional money management services, which until recently catered to institutions and well-heeled individual investors, are quickly being removed, making what one considers to be a prudent investment decision can be daunting. You, the investor, are presented with a myriad of investment services ranging from traditional choices such as mutual funds, unit trusts, and certificates of deposit to finely tuned, specialized niche professional portfolio management services. These rapidly developing and expanding money management services are available to investors with as little as $100,000 in capital to invest. Even these minimum capital hurdles will be lowered over time as new hybrid pooled accounts similar to mutual funds are created.

For whom would these portfolio management services be appropriate? Retirees, small business owners, pension plan managers, widows or widowers, divorcées, estate heirs, savers, and high-income individuals are a few of the candidates who would be well served by the services of America's most sought after and respected independent investment firms. For many investors, managing a relatively large part of one's total net worth is both intimidating and frightening. This is especially true for retirees who are not accustomed to managing money in the volatile capital

markets. You, as an investor, are expected to make sound decisions in a field unrelated to your work experiences. A costly financial mistake at this juncture in life cannot be recouped. With so
much at stake, why take a chance when you can hire the best? By
hiring a good money manager, you should not only improve your
financial condition, but you will also lift a tremendous amount of
stress from your own shoulders.

This book covers the structure, mechanics, and pros and cons of
using professional portfolio management services. Additionally,
10 of America's best money managers, each representing a different approach or style to investing, are highlighted. Their unique
histories, investment philosophies, and specific strategies are detailed. Finally, and most importantly, this book will help you
define and develop your *own* investment profile, personality, or
makeup. Once defined, you may use the guidelines presented to
properly match your risk/return objectives to that of an independent investment manager.

I.   WHY THE EXPLOSIVE GROWTH
OF PROFESSIONAL MONEY
MANAGEMENT SERVICES?

At the writing of this book, over $100 billion had been allocated by
individual investors to money management programs—triple
the amount of just two years ago. Is this another Wall Street fad?
The trends suggest otherwise. At a recent money management
conference, Richard Schilffarth, a brokerage consultant and monitor of money manager investment returns, forecast that in 20 years
assets in individual money management programs will match
those assets invested in mutual funds. He projected that total
assets will total over $1 trillion by the year 2000 and top $3 trillion
in 20 years. Money is pouring in at the five largest brokerage firms
at a rate of $250 million to $500 million per month. Each firm has
opened over 100,000 individual managed accounts.

Obviously, something about these programs has hit the right
nerve among investors, advisers, and the brokerage community.
What are the common experiences among investors and brokers
that have laid the groundwork and created such a demand for

these portfolio management programs? Here are eight of the most obvious reasons behind this astonishing growth rate:

1. Investors and brokers alike are tired of and fed up with "hit and miss" investment strategies in which stocks, bonds, real estate, and/or hard assets are bought and sold with no relation to an overall financial strategy or investment philosophy. They wake up one day and look at their disorganized, inappropriate, unwieldy, crazy-quilt collection of so-called investments and say to themselves, "This does not make any sense. I need some order." In this confusing and upsetting world, investors seek a more serene, prudent, and systematized approach to building and protecting hard-earned, long-term assets.

2. The process, which is covered in detail later in this chapter, induces investors to adopt a disciplined and clearly defined investment style versus chasing the latest hot investment theme or fad. Also, it reorients both you, the investor, and your broker away from the unhealthy behavior of checking the markets and your investments every three seconds, three hours, three days, or three weeks.

3. People understand that no financial guarantees exist and instead desire and accept a more realistic, risk-controlled approach to handling investments.

4. A disciplined and coherent process is established in which due diligence and supervision is emphasized. A financial adviser/ broker, much to the investor's amazement, actually sits down to probe, discuss, and define your investment profile. The broker has completely modified his role to that of a consultant, not a stock, bond, and partnership salesperson. The broker's sole purpose is to correctly identify your risk tolerances and then to make an appropriate match with a manager. Once the relationship between you and the adviser has been established, it is the broker's job to monitor both the money manager and the client to ensure that the client's objectives are being met. Now you and your broker are sitting on the same side of the table, setting your objectives and evaluating the performance of your selected manager.

5. You have access to top-ranked money managers who normally accept accounts with much higher minimums, usually $1 million to $10 million.

6. A well-diversified portfolio is created, thereby eliminating a

common investor error of overconcentration, in which too many assets are allocated to too few securities. Gone are the five stock portfolios which gyrate as much as your EKG. In other words, the temptation to put all your eggs in one basket is negated.

7. Most investors and brokers do not have the time, inclination, or ability to prudently manage a complex and diversified portfolio. We are afraid to face the cold realities that our own investment performance is subpar.

8. Potential conflicts of interest such as churning (actively trading for commissions) are removed.

II.   WRAP-FEE PAYMENT PROGRAMS

No, wrap-fees are not the latest adaptation from the music world to the financial markets. Rather, the wrap-free is a brokerage arrangement whereby you are charged a fixed percentage fee based on total assets under management. This fee covers unlimited client consulting, investment management, performance monitoring, and custodial, commission, and brokerage costs. Included in your consulting is the setting of investment objectives, defining your risk tolerances and continually reviewing these objectives over the course of your lifetime. This fixed percentage runs between 1 percent and 3 percent, depending on the account size, account type (international, domestic, fixed, balanced, equity, and style of management), and portfolio strategies.

Wrap-fees, although the fastest growing, are only one way to pay for investment management services. Other arrangements to compensate for both the manager and broker services include fee *plus* commission and performance-related contracts, but the asset growth under these fee structures pales when compared to the growth of wrap-fee programs.

III.   MUTUAL FUNDS VERSUS MONEY MANAGER SERVICES

What about the use of mutual funds over personal money management services? Both are excellent examples of professional advisory services in which the investor can receive the benefits of top-ranked portfolio management, diversification, and clearly defined investment objectives. Mutual funds are especially appropriate for dollar/value cost averaging and investors with smaller amounts of capital. Examples include monthly investment programs and pension plans in which monthly payroll contributions are made on behalf of the participant.

Generally, owning a mutual fund is less expensive than hiring an independent investment advising firm. According to several leading publications, the average equity fund expense ratio ranges from 1.19 percent to 2.0 percent. But this figure may not include the transaction costs (which are difficult to calculate and run all over the board, depending on the manager's trading style), fund redemptions and purchases, and the state of the markets. Therefore, it is important to analyze the actual expense ratio of a particular fund over an extended period of time such as the last five years.

If you've done your homework on a specific mutual fund, clearly understand and have defined your own risk/return profile, know how to effectively diversify a portfolio, have confidence in a particular fund's manager or style, and continuously monitor both personnel changes and the total return per unit of risk/ volatility, a mutual fund's cost structure can be hard to beat. The reality is, unless you have a substantial amount to invest, hiring an independent portfolio manager to oversee and manage your assets will probably cost you more money than a mutual fund. But if you value the services discussed in this book and/or utilize a manager with an active investment style, then money management services bear consideration. What are some of the common reasons an investor would enlist the services of a portfolio management firm?

A. People Desire to Know What They Own

Some of us enjoy looking at, watching, thinking about, and/or discussing our portfolios. We want to know where we stand and how our portfolios are structured so we can discuss our holdings, what the portfolio managers are thinking, and how our managers are adjusting our portfolios under the current economic scenario. In other words, with properly run portfolio-management programs, we feel like participants instead of just spectators.

B. A Feeling of Safety and Importance Comes with Having Your Account Managed by One of America's Best Portfolio Management Firms

People like both the status and security that comes from having their assets managed by a top-ranked portfolio manager. The author has been amazed by investors' desires to be included in the exclusive $100,000-plus group. (People scrape the bottoms of their piggy banks to get to the magical $100,000 entry level.)

C. Managed Account Investors Don't Have to Bail Out with the Herd

Invariably, there will be market downturns and mini-panics in which unsophisticated retail investors bail out of their stocks. Every year or crisis we see another example. In a managed account, your portfolio manager can "lean against the wind" and buy into these unwarranted drops. During these sell-offs, some mutual fund managers, against their wills, are forced to liquidate securities because of heavy investor redemptions. On numerous occasions, Peter Lynch has described the predicament he faced on October 20, 1987, when the market crashed. He saw it as one of the best buying opportunities of his career for the Fidelity Magellan Fund. But instead, he had to liquidate shares to meet redemption requirements and, therefore, had little cash to invest. Investors were fleeing from rather than taking advantage of the market and his well-run fund. The exceptions to this phenomenon include open-ended mutual funds with long-term–oriented, loyal shareholder groups who refuse to allow market shakeouts to scare them off and closed-end funds where no new money is accepted. In a closed-end fund, changes in ownership occur only through the sale of existing shares and the purchase of these shares on the market exchanges.

D. Managed Account Investors Avoid Unwanted and Unwarranted Tax Liability

Mutual fund holders are at an unfair disadvantage within our tax system due to the fact they can incur tax liability for accumulated gains prior to their owning of the specific fund. When a sale of a specific holding is made within a fund, the tax liability is shared among all *current* shareholders, no matter how long or short a time period they have actually owned the fund. For example, if you purchase and own a fund for one month at the end of a particular tax year, taxes on capital gains and dividends are owed for the fund's entire year of activity. Under the managed account system, because each account is treated independently, taxes are owed only when gains are generated within a portfolio.

E.   Investors Have Special Needs

You may prefer to own no "sin" (alcohol, drug, tobacco, etc.), South African, or nuclear energy company stocks. Or your tax situation may dictate the selling of losers to negate taxable gain liability or winners to cover carryover losses. Or you may have some unusual liquidity or income needs. All of these special desires and needs can be handled within a managed account. This individual portfolio tailoring is very difficult, if not impossible, within the mutual fund structure.

IV.   THE PROCESS

Once you have determined that the services of an independent portfolio advisory firm are appropriate for meeting your financial goals, then it is time to initiate the process. Unless you go directly to the money manager, which is not feasible without a minimum of $1 million to $10 million in capital to invest, the process begins with a meeting with an investment consultant or broker.

A.   The Broker/Consultant's Role

As previewed earlier in this chapter, one of the first and most critical steps in investing is to accurately define your risk/return profile or personality. The consultant/broker is responsible for assisting in analyzing your profile, preparing the investment policy statement, suggesting several independent money managers that suit your needs, and finally, monitoring your account to evaluate the money manager's performance. Part of the fee you pay within a wrap-fee structure covers the cost of this ongoing servicing of the account. This situation differs from the traditional broker/client relationship in which a broker is paid only when transactions occur. Thus, a unique three-way relationship among the client, the broker, and the money manager is formed to help the investor develop, select, and monitor an appropriate investment strategy.

Each money manager has his own particular style and level of risk. Each will vary the amounts and percentages of stocks, bonds, and cash held in a portfolio. You must select a money manager who can vary these percentages to meet specified goals and objectives. Here a personal broker can be immensely helpful.

The importance of aligning your investment philosophy with a selected manager cannot be overemphasized. The money manager's philosophy represents his belief about how best to approach the market. When meeting with an adviser/consultant for the selection, you should answer these questions *before* signing on:

- Does his philosophy make sense to me?
- How was this philosophy developed?
- Does the philosophy represent the way I view the world or the way the manager wants it to be?
- Does it seem to be aggressive, conservative, or middle-of-the-road in terms of risk?
- Do the risk, volatility, and return data meet my objectives?
- Do I feel comfortable with the type of companies and debt instruments in the portfolio?
- If I had the opportunity to meet the manager or his staff, was I comfortable with them?
- Can I live with this investment style over a full business cycle (3–5 years minimum)?
- Would I prefer to use multiple managers/styles that complement each other (value and growth, small and large companies)?

B.   Defining an Investor's Temperament

"In investing money, the amount of investment you want should depend on whether you want to eat well or sleep well."

J. Kenfield Morley, 1937

To assist you in establishing a framework for manager selection, your consultant/broker will invariably ask several questions. These questions are designed to develop a detailed personal investment risk/return profile. In Appendix A a sample list of questions taken from different questionnaires is highlighted. For those who want to do a quick and dirty risk analysis and find the questions listed in the appendix too tedious, cumbersome, or lengthy to answer, Michael Lipper, president of Lipper Analytical Services, has designed a five-question quiz to help you get a *general* reading on your investment temperament. Once you have completed it, tally your score. Although it is not meant to replace the full-blown, extensive questionnaire, this quiz will give you a general idea of your risk tolerance. In other words, the quiz is a good starting point.

1. My investment is for the long term. The end result is more important than how I went about achieving it.
   (1) Totally disagree.
   (2) Can accept variability, but no loss of capital.
   (3) Can accept reasonable amounts of price fluctuation in total return.
   (4) Can accept an occasional year of negative performance in the interest of building capital.
   (5) Agree.
2. What is the importance of current income?
   (1) Essential and must be known.
   (2) Essential, but willing to accept uncertainty about the amount.
   (3) Important, but there are other factors to consider.
   (4) Modest current income is desirable.
   (5) Irrelevant.

3. How much decline can you accept in a single quarter?
   (1) None.
   (2) A little, but not for the entire year.
   (3) Consistency of results is more important then superior returns.
   (4) A few quarters of decline are a small price to pay to be invested when the stock market takes off.
   (5) Unimportant.
4. How important is it to beat inflation?
   (1) Preservation of capital and income are more important.
   (2) I'm willing to beat inflation, but other investment needs come first.
   (3) It's essential to get a real return on my investment.
5. How important is it to beat the stock market over up-and-down economic cycles?
   (1) Irrelevant.
   (2) I prefer consistency.
   (3) Critical.

Total your numbers from each of the five questions. What does your score mean?

5 - Low tolerance for risk.

10 - Moderate risk taker.

25 - You don't mind risks.

Most of us are pulled back and forth between fear and greed. On one hand, we are scared—knowing we don't have the time, expertise, or inclination to manage our funds. You wonder, especially in the new era of low interest rates, whether you will earn enough income to cover your expenses. What if you outlive your savings and investments? Additionally, world events and their ties to the financial markets seem to be getting more complex daily. On the other hand (greed), we want to make as much money as we can. All around us are people who have successfully earned, saved and invested, inherited wealth, or just gotten lucky. Add a lot of help from the media and financial press, and we have trouble breaking out of this fear and greed tug-of-war.

This book will help you, the investor, keep from falling prey to this trap. Yes, 10 of America's best money managers' strategies and track records are presented and detailed to satisfy everyone's greed appetite. But more importantly, this book will help you in developing your *own* investment personality profile and will present some guidelines for matching this profile to an appropriate investment adviser.

To assist you in understanding the differences in investor profiles and why it is critical to allocate investable funds appropriately, an analogy may be helpful. Think of a freeway with three lanes all heading in the same direction. Some investors are wary of even getting on the freeway. They would rather take all the back roads to get from point A to point B. The trip will take four times as long, but at least they are not at risk by driving on the freeway. Investors who have this risk-averse psychological makeup should keep their funds in short-term, insured, or U.S. government-backed securities. Yes, they will earn a menial return and lose purchasing power over time (not stay ahead of inflation), but at least they don't have to worry about the loss of principal.

For those willing to get on the freeway, three choices exist: the conservative right lane, the balanced middle lane, or the more aggressive left lane. Some investors nervously hug the right lane, traveling at 10 miles below the 55 mile-per-hour speed limit. These investors should choose a management style that is bent on capital preservation where the equity exposure is controlled. In addition, a significant percentage of assets should be maintained in short-to-intermediate investment-grade bonds. Two of the more conservative, balanced (in terms of stock, bond, and money market allocations) managers highlighted in this book include Regent Investor Services and Fox Asset Management.

The middle lane, where at least 50 percent of the equity-oriented investment population belongs, is for those willing to accept some risk. However, no attempt is made to "hit the ball over the fence." Those investors who fall into this category have a number of choices including balanced, blue-chip, value, and asset allocation strategies. Examples in this book include Avatar Associates, Systematic Financial Management, Inc., Brandes Investment Management, and Rittenhouse Financial Services.

For those who cannot decide if they belong in the middle or left lanes or who prefer to move back and forth between the two lanes, the more aggressive managers using small- to mid-sized growth and value stocks would be appropriate. Examples in the book include Nicholas-Applegate Capital Management, Harris Bretall Sullivan & Smith, Inc., Roger Engemann & Associates, and Fisher Investments.

If the past is any indication, during bull markets, those traveling in the left lane will cover the most distance (earn the most money), but along the way will be occasionally stopped by a state patrol officer and fined for speeding. In other words, you must be willing to accept the volatility and periodic losses associated with more aggressive growth stocks. For many, a smooth ride is much more important than covering the most distance.

For those who find the left lane to be too passive or slow and would prefer to drive down the median strip, a few suggestions include Las Vegas, the race track, and aggressive options/ commodity trading strategies. Once your investment profile has been clearly defined, an investment policy statement needs to be developed.

V.   DEVELOPING THE INVESTMENT POLICY STATEMENT

From the questions highlighted in Appendix A, not only is your profile detailed so a proper manager match can be made, but this information provides the data necessary to generate a personalized, written *investment policy statement*. The policy statement outlines your objectives, risk parameters, income needs, and the strategies the chosen manager will pursue. This policy statement will also serve as a standard from which you can evaluate future performance (see the sample policy statement in Appendix B).

The policy statement is your set of instructions for the money manager, describing precisely how you wish to have your money managed and what results you expect. It helps prevent misunderstandings over the investments made for you and creates an obligation on the part of both your broker and your money manager to make sure all investments conform to the rules set down in the statement.

An investment policy statement is a good document to have no matter how much money is available for investment. For many years, most major institutional investors have maintained an investment policy statement in order to comply with ERISA (the Employee Retirement Income Security Act of 1974). In recent years, the adoption of these statements has become more widespread among individual investors as well as institutions. The investment policy statement sets forth the following information:

• Statement of purpose—a clear understanding of the relationship between the client and the money manager.

• Investment objectives—the determination of primary and secondary investment objectives, such as safety of principal, preservation of capital, or growth.

• Investment goals—specific methods of comparison to determine investment success; for example, equaling or exceeding certain economic or market indicators such as the consumer price index or the Dow Jones Industrial Average.

• Investment guidelines—any limitations on the quality or nature of investments to be made, such as maintaining a specific percentage of the portfolio in bonds or limiting the percentage committed to common stocks.

• Investment performance review—a periodic (usually quarterly) review of progress in the account.

• Communications—an agreement between the parties describing the nature and timing of communication, such as monthly reports and written confirmations after every trade.

Chapter Two

Selecting a Manager

Upon completion of the all-important investment risk profile work, you can select a specific money manager in accordance with your acknowledged goals, objectives, and risk/volatility tolerances. The 10 profiled managers in this book should make that selection process easier. Yet, why these 10? Here is how the selection was made.

There are over 20,000 registered investment advisers in America. Not only does the sheer number of them confuse most investors, but the bewildering array of investment styles, size of assets under management, and performance track records make any truly informed comparison and selection almost impossible.

And yet almost every day, we read about the latest money manager to have struck it rich with a new investment strategy. You begin to wonder, who are these people who profess to have all the answers? Have they just gotten lucky in the last several years (or the last several weeks!), or are they seasoned and time-tested investors?

Over the years, we have seen many money managers come and go. And we have many times asked ourselves, who are the best money managers in America? Usually, we fail to come up with an answer because we never really defined what is meant by *the best*.

Does the best mean those who made the most money last year? Does it mean those who have never lost money in any year? Does it mean those who are managing the most money for others? Or is *the best* just a term which will change depending on how you look at it? After all, the best investment adviser for me may not be the best for you.

There *is* a way to choose those managers who can be called the best. Simply put, the best money managers in America are those that have demonstrated the highest rates of return with the least risk (volatility).

For instance, if money manager A made 30 percent on your money in one year, you would likely say that he was fairly successful. But, if during that year your portfolio ranged from +70 percent to −70 percent, you might ask whether the risk taken in that roller-coaster year to achieve the 30 percent gain was worth it. A fundamental question any investor should ask when reviewing a manager's volatility and performance record is, "Following a portfolio value decline, how long does it take, on average, to get my money back?" This helps prevent a common occurrence in which an investor enlists the services of a highly successful but volatile manager, has two down quarters, and then spends the next two years just trying to get back to even.

Likewise, if money manager B made a lesser rate of return on your money in the same year, let's say 20 percent, but your portfolio increased steadily during each successive month, you might be willing to accept the lower return for the lower risk. You might even say that, despite the lower return, money manager B did a better job because he had less risk and yet was still able to provide you with a good profit.

In writing this book, I compared the money managers' rates of return with how much risk they took to achieve those returns. Technically, statistical measures such as standard deviations, Sharpe ratios, and raw performance data were used to analyze money managers' track records. The true test of money managers was how much added performance they could pack into their return per unit of risk.

The scattergram has become the most widely used tool in relating risk to return. Virtually all consultants use this technique in their assessment of investment advisers. If you have seen any literature from brokerage houses or investment consultants comparing investment advisers, you have no doubt seen a variation of the graph depicted in Exhibit 2–1.

The scattergram is easy to understand. First, the Y-axis (vertical and with the scale on the left) is the annualized rate of return of the money manager's portfolio. In Exhibit 2–1, for example, manager 1 has achieved a 12.60 percent compounded rate of return over the five-year period ended March 31, 1992. Second, the X-axis (horizontal and with the scale at the bottom) is a measurement of the risk of the money manager's portfolio.

EXHIBIT 2–1
Blended Risk/Return Analysis (For Five Years Ending March 31, 1992)

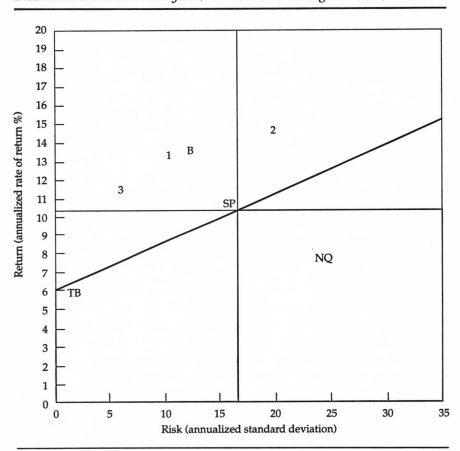

Source: Prudential Securities Investment Management & Consulting Research.

Risk may be measured in different ways. In preparing this book, alphas, betas, and a host of other statistical methods of assessing risk were examined. The alpha calculation measures a specific portfolio manager's relative value added above a given market index, such as U.S. Treasury bills, the Standard & Poor's 500 and/or a blended index. The beta calculation measures the amount of market risk the manager has taken in comparison to the market itself.

While all these methods are valuable in making risk evaluations, the two most powerful, intuitively understandable, and widely used statistical measuring tools are standard deviation and the Sharpe ratio. The Sharpe ratio calculates the amount of return per unit of risk the manager generated over or under the riskless T-bill return. This helps you determine how much value your manager added. Standard deviation is a statistical method of measuring the volatility or range of returns for any given time period. To explain and illustrate the concepts, the return and volatility figures of three of the managers reviewed in the book—Rittenhouse Financial Services, Nicholas-Applegate Capital Management, and Regent Investor Services—are used in Exhibit 2–1. (The choice of these three managers does not indicate any bias of the author. Any of the 10 managers could have been used to explain the concepts.)

Rittenhouse Financial Services (manager 1 in Exhibit 2–1) has return and volatility risk figures (standard deviation calculations) over the five-year period ending March 31, 1992, of 12.20 percent and 10.60 percent, respectively. These calculations are annualized figures based on quarterly numbers. These numbers indicate that about 95 percent of the time Rittenhouse's past return has fallen within 10.60 percentage points on either side of the 12.20 percent annualized return, assuming that the numbers are normally distributed. Adding and subtracting 10.60 to and from 12.20 percent gives us a band of returns of 1.60 percent to 22.80 percent. The 95 percent figure is used because we ran the numbers from Exhibit 2–1 out to two standard deviations. Had we used one standard deviation, then we could assume that two thirds (66 percent) of the time the returns fall within the calculated band. Three standard deviations would give us a 99 percent confidence level, again assuming the figures are normally distributed.

The same calculations can be made for Nicholas-Applegate (manager 2) and Regent Investor Services (manager 3). With Nicholas-Applegate, clients earned a 14 percent annual return for the five years ending March 31, 1992, with a standard deviation of 22.80 percent, which means that the band of returns for 95 percent of the time period measured is minus 8.80 percent to positive 36.80 percent. For Regent Investor Services, the return of 11.10 percent is approximately 30 percent lower than Nicholas-Applegate's for the five-year period, but the volatility (6.9 percent) is less than one third of Nicholas-Applegate's—which highlights the trade-off investors need to evaluate and accept. For Regent, the band of returns for 95 percent of the time is much narrower—4.20 percent to 18.00 percent. In other words, for those seeking a steadier, less volatile/risky return with the trade-off of lower returns, a manager like Regent would be appropriate. For those who are willing to accept higher risk/volatility levels in search of higher returns, a growth stock manager such as Nicholas-Applegate would fit the bill. Rittenhouse's past risk and reward characteristics place it between Nicholas-Applegate and Regent Investor Services.

The Ibbotson Associates study covering broad asset classes from 1926 through 1991 showed common stocks, when compared to long-term bonds and short-term investments, incurred the most single-year volatility or range of returns. Yet, this band of volatility is narrowed over time *plus* the potential for negative returns is reduced dramatically (see Exhibit 2–2). In other words, this study supports the case for taking a long-term stock market perspective.

When evaluating a money manager, it is important to eyeball the quarterly performance numbers over a five- to ten-year period so you will obtain an idea of the range of returns. Pay special attention to the down quarters. Once you have analyzed both the good and bad periods and the potential drawdowns, then you need to ask yourself one simple question: can I live with these fluctuations and variable returns?

By plotting both the actual return and the standard deviation on the same graph and calculating the Sharpe ratios, you can see how each manager has fared against its competition. In other words, all these money managers are now placed on the same playing field and therefore can be fairly judged.

The line on the graph connecting the Treasury bill rate (indicated by 3) with the return on the Standard & Poor's 500 (indicated by 1) is called the *Capital Markets Line* or the *Efficient Frontier*. This line shows you that for each unit of incremental risk incurred, one should expect to be rewarded with a higher unit of return. This result is what you should have achieved without using a money manager. If your money manager has added value to your investments, he or she will fall above this line.

In judging money managers, you should look for a consistent pattern of outperforming the competition and capital markets/efficient frontier line. By using the statistical techniques of stan-

EXHIBIT 2–2
Asset Class Volatility and the Impact of Time on Your Investments

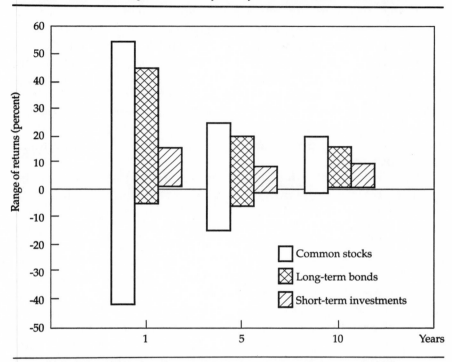

Source: Prudential Securities Investment Management and Consulting Research.

dard deviation and Sharpe ratios, you are able to apply the same standard of comparison to all money managers. This is why the scattergram is so useful. It allows one to make apple-to-apple comparisons. The risk/reward method of comparison is a discipline that has been used by institutional and wealthy investors for many years.

A word of warning regarding the reporting of investment advisory performance: in order to ensure you are not making an apples-to-oranges comparison when evaluating multiple managers, you need to know whether the rates of return are reported after the deduction of all the fees and costs associated with the management of an investment portfolio. Some managers report *net/net* numbers, which means they have deducted all fees, while others report *gross* performance figures, which are calculated prior to the deduction of any fees and costs. Other investment advisers report *net* numbers, which are one step closer to actual client returns. In net reporting, all commissions and transaction costs are deducted, but the reported performance figure does not include a deduction for the advisory fee. In other words, to obtain a true performance number, one needs to deduct all costs to accurately compare different money managers. The numbers reported and used for examples in Exhibit 2–1 and throughout the book are institutional reported numbers and therefore are net figures (net of all commissions and transaction fees and gross of money managers' advisory fees).

The selection of the top money managers for this book was the result of this risk/reward concept. Also required was that each money manager in this survey accept a minimum $100,000 account through any of the major and regional brokerage houses that offer these programs. The $100,000 minimum requirement eliminated many managers who had excellent track records but were available to only the well-heeled individual or institutional investor. This additional screening process was beneficial for several reasons. First, all the performance track records have been checked and monitored by these major brokerage houses to ensure that the money managers have indeed produced the returns that they claim. Second, all the money managers have undergone scrutiny by these major brokerage firms as viable business enterprises. For example, all have a minimum of $100 million of assets under management; all have been in business for a minimum of five years; and all have at least three individual portfolio managers at the firm who have successfully managed clients' assets for a minimum 10-year period. This is the due diligence work required by most fiduciaries.

The investment advisers' integrity, philosophy, communications, trading and research capabilities, fiscal stability, and decision-making processes all have important weightings in the final analysis. As Seth A. Klarman, money manager and author of the book *At the Margin of Safety: Going Beyond Financial Myth-Making to Find Real Investment Values* and *Barron's* article "Do They Eat at Home?—Guides to Choosing a Money Manager," points out, "The law of probability tells us that almost anyone can achieve phenomenal success over any quick measurement period. It is the task of those evaluating a money manager to ascertain how much of the past is due to luck and how much to skill." Remember, a manager's short-term performance is style driven (i.e., whether the manager's style is in or out of favor). You have no guarantees that the 10 highlighted managers in this book will continue to lead the pack over the next decade. You should keep reminding yourself of Henry Ford's advice when we begin to "giggle and gaw" over a manager's past track record—"History is bunk!"

I.   EVALUATING ONGOING MANAGER PERFORMANCE

How do you know you've made the correct manager selection and asset allocation? It is sometimes very obvious—when the market takes its first predictable retraction. If you panic, act overly concerned, and so forth, then a red light should go on in your head. Your assets should be risked only to the point that you sleep well at night. If the nightly stock market analyst reports that the Dow dropped 50 points today and your stomach starts to turn, you know that your equity allocation is too concentrated. Another sign: if watching the market starts interfering with your daily, enjoyable activities. For example, if you start catching yourself turning on CNN throughout the day because you're worried about the market, then you may want to consider using a less aggressive investment style.

Once a quarter you should ask yourself five simple questions:

1. Did the performance meet your return and risk objectives?
2. How did these results compare to the market average or indices?
3. Was there anything unusual or any extenuating circumstances (positive or negative) that may have impacted the short-term performance?
4. Have your objectives changed?
5. When reviewing the manager's written outlook, does it seem to make sense and fit what you want done with your funds?

On a quarterly basis, the investor will receive a number of charts and figures to assist in analyzing the performance. In Appendix C, sample charts are depicted along with brief explanations of each. Included are bar, bull and bear, accumulated value, and scatter-gram charts for you to review and study.

II. SUMMARY OF INTRODUCTORY MATERIAL

In conclusion, the most important decision is not which manager and investment style you should follow, but how do you make the best match between your objectives and the adviser's investment philosophy, strategy, and style. Concentrating on performance figures and the winners over the past couple of years is not recommended. In fact, most savvy investors use a contrarian approach, placing capital with those managers whose last few years' returns have lagged these market averages. Simply put, starting with performance is putting the cart before the horse. Each person has what I call an *investment personality* which covers his or her outlook toward the world, return expectations, risk tolerances, stomach for volatility, and so on. When a broker asks you a question regarding your risk tolerances, for example, it is an attempt to develop your profile so an appropriate match can be made. When an inappropriate match is made, the results can be disastrous. If you are comfortable with the manager's discipline and style, then you are much less apt to make poor, ill-informed, emotional decisions. After reviewing a specific manager's style and track record, you should be able to answer these four simple questions:

1. How does the manager go about selecting investments?
2. Does the selection system make sense?
3. Are you comfortable with the approach?
4. Can you live with the historical risk-adjusted returns, knowing that although these will not exactly replicate themselves, they will give you a general idea of what to expect?

In addition, the type of securities purchased and the trading style tells a lot about the adviser. Does the manager seek undervalued stocks, or is he a buyer of the faster moving and growing companies? Does he employ a strict sell strategy like using sell-stop-orders, or does he hold through thick or thin? Is he looking for the next Microsoft, or is he looking for the turnaround of a fallen giant of yesteryear? Again, you should be drawn to and feel very comfortable with the investment adviser's investment discipline. In other words, your investment viewpoints should be similar. A well-informed consultant/broker should be able to assist you in this determination.

Enough said—let us get to the meat of the book—the histories, philosophies, and strategies of 10 of America's best money managers. You will find, after reading one or two of the manager chapters, that you will be drawn to a particular investment style. That is, the manager's investment style is congruent with your objectives and outlook. This agreement should be a natural outgrowth and is important because you are more likely to make good, nonemotional decisions if you are comfortable with the overall strategies being employed with your money. The intention of this book is *not* to make the investment decision for you, but to give you the necessary information to assist you in recognizing the differences in money managers and to help you make the important decision of managing your money a little easier. Objective, rational decisions should be made by a manager who has the resources and knowledge to focus on the variables impacting today's marketplace and, most importantly, your hard-earned assets.

Chapter 3

Avatar Associates
The Big Mistake Avoider

"Don't fight the Fed."
"Don't fight the tape."
"Beware of the crowd."
"Cut your losses early and let your profits run."

Martin Zweig-isms

Although many investment advisers, and investors as well, recite this commonplace investment jargon, few have the discipline to put it into practice. Avatar Associates is one manager that uses these popular maxims as a prescription for successful portfolio management.

Avatar, from the Hindu term meaning "the living incarnate of a god" (a god that has come back in a recognizable, living form) was cofounded and continues to be comanaged by the popular *Wall Street Week* panelist Martin E. Zweig and Edward S. Babbitt, Jr. Both men wear many hats successfully. Zweig, in addition to acting as Avatar's director of research, publishes the top-ranked *Zweig Forecast* market newsletter for the short-term-oriented, do-it-yourself investor/trader and manages several closed-end and open-end mutual funds. Babbitt, while leaving the asset allocation and timing decisions to Zweig, oversees all day-to-day portfolio decisions, as well as handling all of Avatar's organizational activities.

A quick review of Avatar's enviable performance during the 1980s is important. For the 10-year period 1981–90, Avatar's equity and cash portfolios outperformed the S&P 500 with only a 68 percent stock market exposure (32 percent less risk than a fully invested position). For five years (1987–91), Avatar's track record was compared to an independent SEI corporation scattergram (Exhibit 3–1) comprised of 135 well-regarded money managers. The message is simple and straightforward—Avatar outperformed the median stock money manager with considerably less risk.

This performance was not a result of Avatar hitting home runs with its clients' funds, but of making correct asset allocations. In fact, Avatar's portfolio style is often categorized by investment manager consultants as *tactical asset allocation*.

Tactical asset allocation (TAA), a mouthful for most investors, is a sophisticated version of market timing. TAA is a highly quantitative approach in which Avatar attempts to measure the relative risks and potential returns of stocks, bonds, and cash (money market funds), and continually adjusts client portfolios accordingly. Charles M. White, one of Avatar's principals and key portfolio managers, defines Avatar's version of TAA with these comments: "Basically, we try to measure risk in the stock and bond markets. When risk rises, we sell our stocks and bonds, and when risk falls, we increase our clients' exposure to stocks and bonds." This portfolio flexibility and willingness to let indicators, not emotions, dictate overall strategy are hallmarks of Avatar's success.

I.   HISTORY OF AVATAR— BEDROOM BEGINNINGS

Avatar Associates was formed in the second bedroom of Babbitt's apartment after he had struggled in 1969 as a stockbroker at E. F. Hutton & Company. Zweig, while teaching at the nearby New York City Bernard Baruch College, was initiating his fledgling investment newsletter, the *Zweig Forecast*. Babbitt, who had been schooled as a Harvard M.B.A. in the Graham & Dodd investment philosophy (buy stocks when they are undervalued, wait for the rest of the investment community to bid the share prices higher, and then sell your shares for a nice profit) became disenchanted with this investment methodology when no one told him what to do when your stock prices took a dive. Babbitt painfully recalled,

EXHIBIT 3-1

Past 5-Years Gross Annualized Equity Account Performance and Risk,
1987–1991 (Period Ending December 31, 1991)

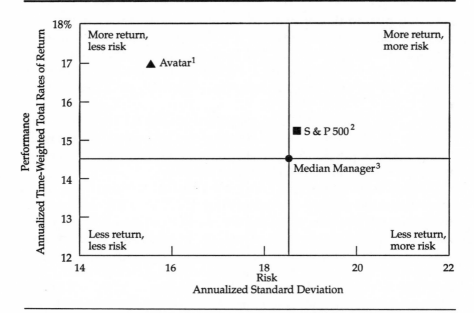

[1] The Avatar performance composite is the mean time-weighted total rates of return (which includes the reinvestment of all dividends and interest plus any realized and unrealized gain or loss) of all discretionary institutional tax-exempt equity (stocks and cash) accounts over $1 million from January 1, 1987–June 30, 1989. Beginning on July 1, 1989, the composite includes all discretionary Select Managers equity portfolios managed by Avatar Associates. Avatar Associates makes no warranty of the accuracy of the performance data compiled by the Select Managers program.

The performance composite is compiled in accordance with the methods set forth by the Bank Administration Institute (BAI) and the Association for Investment Management and Research (AIMR), except that individual accounts are equally weighted instead of dollar-weighted.

The performance composite is calculated using quarterly rates of return which are linked to compute the annual figures which, in turn, are linked to compute the 5-year annualized compound rate of return. Closed accounts are included for each full quarter prior to their closing. Various market indexes and performance benchmarks are used to indicate the investment environment existing during the period measured. Past performance is no guarantee of future results.

For the period from January 1, 1987–June 30, 1989, the Avatar gross performance figure excludes the management fee paid by the client for investing the portfolio, but includes all other costs and expenses, including brokerage commissions. For the period beginning July 1, 1989, the Avatar gross performance figure excludes the single wrap-fee paid by the client for the investment management of his account, the brokerage commissions incurred, and all other costs and expenses of administering a Select Managers portfolio.

[2] Representative stock market performance index.

[3] Representative universe of equity portfolio manager rates of return compiled by SEI Corp.

I did my best fundamental analysis and found a stock to be a good bargain at $50/share, only to find it priced at $40/share before my clients received their buy confirmations. A month later it was $30/share and heading lower. In accordance with the classic Graham & Dodd theory, if the fundamentals remain intact, you buy more. At $20/share my clients figured they had lost enough capital and wanted to bail out of the market completely. In 1969 the Dow Jones Industrial Average declined from 960 to 660, and most of my clients wished they'd never heard of Babbitt's undervalued style of investing.

Bloody and bruised, Babbitt quit his job as a stockbroker to set up his own investment advisory firm with a new set of market indicators. After reading a *Barron's* article written by Zweig using investor pessimism and optimism for asset allocation decisions, Babbitt called Zweig. Expecting a graying professor with years of academic experience, Babbitt instead found a 28-year-old professor of finance eager to apply his newly developed asset allocation models to the real world. Zweig, like Babbitt, was keenly interested in preserving clients' capital in down markets. He had watched his own parents' net worth rise and fall precipitously in the Cleveland real estate market in the 1920s and 1930s. With Babbitt's three remaining clients and Zweig's 13 newsletter subscribers, they formed a long-standing friendship and partnership. It was in Babbitt's apartment that Avatar's investment philosophy and key indicators were first put to real-world use.

During the early years, the stock and bond markets provided few opportunities for Babbitt and Zweig. In fact, during the 1973–74 bear market, the overall stock market declined approximately 38 percent, while Avatar was able to limit client portfolio losses to roughly 16 percent. Although pleased with the firm's relative performance, many of Avatar's clients found plain vanilla U.S. Treasury bills to be a safer bet. Approximately 50 percent of assets under management left Avatar prematurely for safer, lower-yielding accounts. Had those clients exhibited a little patience, they would have seen their Avatar-managed accounts more than double in value from 1975 to 1980.

From its humble beginnings 22 years ago, Avatar has grown to a highly respected portfolio management firm with close to $4.5 billion in assets under management. With a consistent performance record and under the skillful marketing leadership of

Bruce L. Poliquin, director of client services, Avatar's assets under management have increased 10-fold over the past 10 years. This success has allowed Babbitt and Zweig to share the ownership of Avatar with six key employees and maintain a staff of 7 portfolio managers, 5 client servicing professionals, 3 securities traders, 13 operations personnel, and 8 support staff.

II.   PHILOSOPHY—AVOID THE BIG MISTAKE

Avatar's investment philosophy can be best summed up as "avoid the big mistake!" Extreme care is taken to preserve capital. Its portfolio managers realize the importance of protecting money in down markets over outperforming the markets during strong or bullish periods. Avatar believes that investors are not comfortable riding a roller coaster with their nest eggs. The orientation toward reducing portfolio volatility distinguishes Avatar from other investment advisers. Growth is Avatar's goal, but the firm recognizes that preserving capital during difficult markets is a critical factor in achieving long-term investment success.

Avatar's equity and cash accounts have underperformed the averages during the bull market phases, but greatly outperformed the market during those gut-wrenching down markets. Babbitt commented on the results: "We don't like to lose money, so we try to be very protective in down markets. If we are going to make a mistake, I want that mistake to be made while holding too much cash and watching the market go up, rather than holding too much stock and seeing the market go down." Zweig added, "I've been in the markets for over 30 years, and my whole reason for being is to reduce client portfolio volatility. During this time, I've tried to develop a risk-averse style where we participate in the rising markets. But I don't want to be a pig. We try to make a reasonable rate of return in the up markets and not get chewed up in the down markets."

Avatar believes stock and bond selection is secondary to this much bigger question: should you be in the market at all? If so, how much market exposure or risk should be assumed under the current capital market environment? Over the past 20 years,

Avatar's equity plus cash portfolios have been 100 percent invested 12 times and have been 100 percent in cash (money market) only 7 times. Ned Babbitt backed his past portfolio positioning with this comment: "Eighty percent of our success stems from being on the right side of the market. The other 20% results from proper industry and individual security selection."

III.   STRATEGY—THE TREND IS YOUR FRIEND

Rather than attempt to forecast the market's direction, which Avatar Associates believes is impossible, its portfolio managers let the market trends dictate the portfolio strategies ("the trend is your friend"). It sounds simple enough, but why can't the general investor or broker successfully follow market trends? Unlike Avatar, the general investing public tends to get *whipsawed*—buying stocks at the top and selling at the bottom. This phenomenon is highlighted in Exhibit 3–2, where the emotional approach to investing (whipsaw effect) is contrasted with Avatar's style.

This whipsawing occurs for three reasons. The general investing public:

1. Fails to spot early and meaningful changes taking place in the stock and bond markets.

2. Is slow to act *or* waits for confirmation of its beliefs once a change is noted (waits until the market makes a big move up or down and then hops on the bandwagon—a guaranteed pathway to disaster).

3. Allows the fragile human psyche, which constantly needs affirmation, to get in the way of making prudent investment decisions. It is so hard to admit when you are wrong and even harder to act upon it. When investment portfolio value starts heading south, investors fail to stop the hemorrhaging through a disciplined tactic of weeding out the losers. Instead, investors attempt to convince themselves that the decline is not warranted: the market is wrong, the company's troubles are temporary, the earnings really weren't all that bad, and so forth.

EXHIBIT 3–2
The Emotional Approach versus Avatar's Approach to Investing

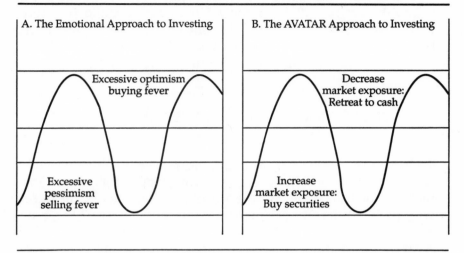

A. The Emotional Approach to Investing

Excessive optimism,
buying fever

Excessive
pessimism
selling fever

B. The AVATAR Approach to Investing

Decrease
market exposure:
Retreat to cash

Increase
market exposure:
Buy securities

IV. PORTFOLIO TACTICS—THREE SIMPLE STEPS

As shown in Exhibit 3–3, Avatar strives to implement its philosophy through a three-step strategy: (1) portfolio asset mix; (2) stock/bond selection; and (3) risk control.

A. Step 1: Portfolio Asset Allocation

Avatar believes the key to portfolio asset mix shifts lies in continually measuring the risk level in the market and gradually reducing exposure when it is rising. This is done by selling stocks/bonds and going into interest-bearing cash equivalents, such as money market instruments. Using the analogy of a poker game, Zweig believes, "one doesn't have to play every hand. When the probabilities are not in your favor, pass and wait for the next hand. The game will still be there tomorrow." When risk is falling, stock holdings are increased, and bond maturities are lengthened to

EXHIBIT 3–3
Investment Strategy

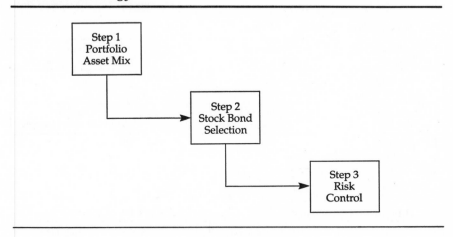

capitalize on growth opportunities. The Avatar portfolio management team moves stock and bond positions in small increments. If a trend has not been recognized—or a trend changes—the flexibility to make adjustments quickly has been retained.

Avatar uses close to 60 quantitative market indicators to direct its portfolio stock/bond/cash mix shifts. These indicators and their respective weightings, which are grouped into three basic categories, are outlined and described in Exhibits 3–4 and 3–5.

1. Economic liquidity (55 percent weighting)—don't fight the Fed. How much money is there in the economy? Assessing money flows or liquidity in the overall system is a key factor in its evaluation. When liquidity is low and the Federal Reserve is tightening (raising interest rates), it's usually a high-risk period in the stock and bond markets. When rates are low and the Fed is loosening (lowering interest rates), it's usually a low-risk period. To determine current monetary conditions, Avatar's staff looks at indicators such as the trend of interest rates, money supply growth, loan demand, debt levels, industrial production, and commodity prices. Simply stated, the best stock market returns over the past 20 years have occurred when the liquidity data

EXHIBIT 3–4
Step 1: Portfolio Asset Mix

Goal: Measure Stock/Bond Market Risk

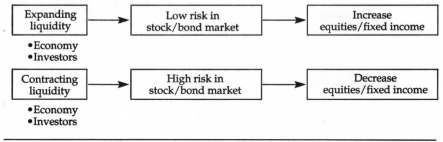

was flashing a low-risk signal. Conversely, when Avatar's liquidity research showed high risk, the S&P 500 had an average decline of over 25 percent per year.

2. **Investor liquidity (30 percent weighting)—beware of the crowd.** What degree of optimism or pessimism are investors, traders, and advisers demonstrating? The attitudes of individual and institutional investors, domestically and globally, are an important factor in determining levels of market risk. Avatar evaluates investor sentiment/attitude by looking at levels of cash sitting in short-term investments such as money market funds, certificates of deposit, and Treasury bills. If cash reserves have been built up (expanding liquidity), many investors are bearish on the market and have already done much of their selling. This usually means low risk. On the other hand, if people are optimistic about the market and have committed their cash reserves to stocks/ bonds, there's less fuel to sustain the market. This converts to a higher-risk environment due to constricting liquidity.

3. **Market momentum (15 percent weighting)—don't fight the tape.** Which way is the market moving? How strong/ weak is this momentum? Superior returns are achieved by being on the right side during major moves. Because Avatar's management doesn't believe in swimming against the tide, it aligns its portfolios with the trend of the market in order to stay out of

EXHIBIT 3–5
How to Measure Stock Market Risk

Stock Liquidity Model		
■ *Economic Liquidity*		*55 Percent Weight*
• Interest rate trends	• Loan demand	
• Fed policy	• Banking liquidity	
• Yield spreads	• Inflation variables	
• Equity valuation		
■ *Investor Liquidity*		*30 Percent Weight*
• Institutional cash levels		
• Retail optimism/pessimism		
• Foreign buying/selling		
■ *Stock Market Momentum*		*15 Percent Weight*
• Short-term trend		

trouble. The goal is to lower overall risk by being in harmony with the long-term trend of the market, which forces the firm to cut back if the market itself starts to act poorly. Market momentum variables measured by the Avatar strategists include the number of stocks advancing versus the number declining, new highs versus new lows in individual securities, and the performance of the market averages, such as S&P 500, Dow Jones Industrial Average, and Value Line index.

Zweig described the market momentum concept in simple terms:

> We try to get in gear with the market. When conditions get lousy, we cut back, and when conditions improve, we buy. This momentum model gave Avatar the sell signal just before Labor Day of 1987, less than two months before the crash, and turned positive in mid-November, one month after the October wipeout. The momentum component of our model was bearish for 800 of the 1,000 point decline. The only problem with utilizing market momentum is that you can get whipsawed in a seesaw type of market. But we'd rather take a whipsaw any day over losing money in a severe bear market or missing out on a big upmove during a bull market.

Avatar's strategies work best when the stock and bond markets have a definite direction (in well-defined bull or bear markets). Avatar does not perform as well in trendless markets. For example, if the stock market trend starts upward (thus signaling to Avatar to increase its clients' equity exposure) and then abruptly declines, Avatar's discipline requires a quick reversal whereby securities are liquidated. Historically, the market has a definite trend—up or down—75 percent of the time, which means Avatar may be out of sync 25 percent of the time.

The portfolio managers continually adjust the stock and bond exposure in accordance with their indicators. While many investors and professional advisers were seriously hurt during the crash of October 1987, Avatar adeptly maneuvered around this climactic event for an exceptional 19.6 percent gain during 1987 for their average balanced account (before deduction of their management fee). As the asset allocation indicators dictate, Avatar reduced the stock exposure in 1987 from 65 percent in January to under 20 percent by the time of the crash in October, and then back to 65 percent in December. Overall, Avatar does not attempt to pick the highs or lows. Rather, its portfolio managers work to capture most of an advance and to avoid most of a decline. Bruce Poliquin explained, "As in football, the best offense is a great defense. Our objective is to catch 70 to 80 percent of a market's upside while avoiding 60 percent or so of the downside. In other words, we strive to participate in, not necessarily outperform, rising stock and bond markets."

B.   Step 2: Stock/Bond Selection

Which stocks should its clients own? Here Avatar looks at fundamental data such as price/earnings, price/book, and price/dividend ratios. With its extensive computer systems, Avatar screens 6,000 stocks to develop a list of 1,000 purchase candidates that meet trading volume requirements (there has to be enough daily trading volume to easily move in and out of a particular security without impacting the price).

These 1,000 candidates are screened for earnings growth over the past five years (the more, the better); earnings momentum (the current quarter versus a quarter one year ago); the analysts' esti-

EXHIBIT 3–6
Quantitative Stock Screens

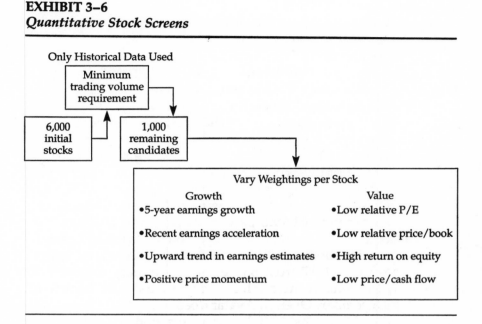

mates (earnings should be better than the analysts' predictions and estimates should be rising—otherwise stock prices tend to underperform over the next six months); relative valuation (which stocks with positive earnings variables offer the best value for the money); and finally, price momentum of the individual securities (stocks that are performing well tend to continue moving upward).

This stock selection process has been in place since 1976. The *Zweig Performance Ratings Report*, using these measurement variables, has been ranked near the top for performance and risk-adjusted rate of return over the past 10 years. From the initial list of 6,000 stocks, Avatar's portfolio managers narrow their buy list to 130 stocks. The quantitative stock screen is summarized in Exhibit 3–6. Similar to its asset allocation strategy, strict disciplines are adhered to.

Consistent with the big mistake avoidance, Avatar's portfolios are among the most diversified (50–70 individual issues per portfolio—see Appendix B). The portfolio managers shift between

EXHIBIT 3–7
Quantify Stock Market Risk

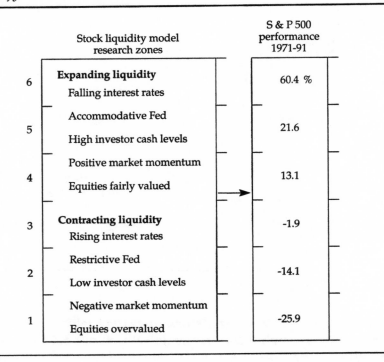

	Stock liquidity model research zones	S & P 500 performance 1971-91
6	**Expanding liquidity** Falling interest rates	60.4 %
5	Accommodative Fed High investor cash levels	21.6
4	Positive market momentum Equities fairly valued	13.1
3	**Contracting liquidity** Rising interest rates	-1.9
2	Restrictive Fed Low investor cash levels	-14.1
1	Negative market momentum Equities overvalued	-25.9

growth and value stock characteristics, depending on the outlook of their market risk and return characteristics. If Avatar's economic liquidity model variables are more positive, growth characteristics are emphasized, and if liquidity begins to contract, then value (low PE/asset-rich) companies are purchased for client portfolios.

Economic liquidity, as described on page 31, receives the most attention and weighting (55 percent in the overall model). According to Avatar, it is the single biggest influence on stock price direction. As highlighted in Exhibit 3–7, for the past 20 years (1971–91) the S&P 500 has generated excess returns when the liquidity model reaches the highest rating within Avatar's research zones. In other words, generally the stock market performs well when interest rates are falling, the Federal Reserve is in an accommodating mode, investor cash levels are high, the stock market

EXHIBIT 3–8
How to Measure Bond Market Risk

Bond Liquidity Model	
■ *Economic Liquidity*	*35 Percent Weight*
• Interest rate trends	
• Yield spreads	
• Fed policy	
■ *Inflation Variables*	*30 Percent Weight*
• Commodity price trends	
• Unemployment claims	
• Industrial production growth	
■ *Bond Market Momentum*	*30 Percent Weight*
• Short-term trend	
■ *Investor Liquidity*	*5 Percent Weight*
• Market vane sentiment	

momentum is positive, and stock prices are fairly valued or not excessively overvalued. Conversely, when interest rates are rising, the Federal Reserve is restricting money supply growth, investors are fully invested in the market and therefore have little sideline cash, the market momentum is negative, and equity prices are overvalued, the S&P 500 performance tends to be poor.

In terms of bond selections, Avatar tends to stay with short- to intermediate-maturity U.S. Treasuries. Defensive by design, Avatar believes that the stock market subjects its clients to enough risk and is satisfied with incremental returns and some capital appreciation with the bond positions.

Similar to varying the growth versus value characteristics for equities, Avatar relies on its proprietary asset allocation research to determine when to change the duration/maturity of its fixed-income holdings. Avatar uses the economic liquidity indicators described in Exhibit 3–8.

Overall, Avatar attempts to increase the amount of money in its system whether the interest rate trend is up, down, or neutral.

EXHIBIT 3–9
Quantify Bond Market Risk

Bond liquidity model research zones		LB G/C performance 1971-91	Commercial paper performance 1971-91
Low 5 risk	**Expanding liquidity**	33.4 %	8.5 %
	Falling interest rates		
	Accommodative Fed		
4	Easing inflation	15.5	8.4
	Positive market momentum		
	Increasing investor pessimism		
3		6.9	8.3
	Contracting liquidity		
	Rising interest rates		
2	Restrictive Fed	-0.5	8.7
	Rising inflation		
	Negative market momentum		
High 1 risk	Increasing investor optimism	-13.9	9.3

Based on its liquidity ratings (Exhibit 3–9), Avatar purchases inter-mediate government bonds when its model signals a low risk rating. Conversely, short-term U.S. Treasury bills are picked when Avatar evaluates the bond market environment as hazard-ous to investors' health. As Exhibit 3–9 demonstrates, there has been a direct correlation between Avatar's risk/liquidity ratings and the relative performance of the bond markets.

C. Step 3: Risk Control Discipline

Knowing when to sell a stock/bond is more difficult than knowing when to buy. Avatar controls portfolio risk by employing three strict sell disciplines. A stock or bond is sold if:

1. The sale is necessary to reduce the portfolio stock/bond exposure.

2. The current market/economic environment dictates a portfolio shift in the bond maturities and/or requires an emphasis on growth or value stocks.
3. A stock price falls by a specific amount.

V. SUMMARY

Avatar is a worrywart's favorite portfolio manager. As Mark Hulbert, editor of the highly regarded *Hulbert Financial Digest*, stated in his November 13, 1989, *Forbes* column, "The smart, steely-nerved investor will shrug off mini-crashes . . . but, how many of us are steely-nerved?"

Volatility keeps most investors on the sidelines. While the market, in general, accurately prices stock and bonds, Avatar believes there are opportunities available for those investors who can adeptly move between asset classes when market inefficiencies occur. TAA, although attractive as a conceptual strategy, is very difficult to put into practice. TAA is a risky strategy for the amateur investor because the investor has to consistently be right on both entry and exit (buy and sell) decisions. Additionally, an improper asset class selection or poor timing can lead to disastrous portfolio results. Avatar is one of the few firms to have successfully implemented TAA. Avatar has not sacrificed client portfolio returns by focusing on risk control. Avatar's balanced (stocks/bonds/cash) accounts have greatly exceeded inflation and comfortably ranked within the top 25 percent of U.S. balanced managers.

The 1980s rewarded investors who practiced a buy-and-hold strategy. This decade may require a completely different style of portfolio management. Avatar feels the 1990s will bring a premium on selecting portfolio managers whose asset allocation tactics will, first, preserve capital on the downside and, second, perform reasonably well on the upside. If you are such an investor who desires an active TAA style, Avatar's approach may be just the right choice for you.

Chapter Four

Brandes Investment Partners, Inc.
The Global Bargain Hunters

Most serious investors and investment advisers have read Benjamin Graham's *The Intelligent Investor* and *Security Analysis* (coauthored with David Dodd), but not more than a handful of people can say they were tutored by the master himself. Charles H. Brandes is one such fortunate person. And how did Brandes put himself into a position to learn from the guru of value investing? How about a little luck!

I. HISTORY AND PHILOSOPHY—MEETING THE GURU OF VALUE INVESTING

After receiving his degree in economics in 1965 from Bucknell University in Pennsylvania, completing a stint as an army officer in 1965–66, and finishing graduate work in business at San Diego State University from 1967 to 1968, Brandes joined a New York Stock Exchange firm in 1968 where he worked as a registered representative, institutional salesman, and research analyst until the birth of his own firm. At that time, the so-called go-go era stocks were flying high. Less than a year after starting his investment career, Brandes watched the Nifty 50 (i.e., go-go stocks) crash and burn in the severe stock market decline of 1969–70. Badly burned from the hypergrowth fire, he was more than ready to learn from these mistakes and open himself to a new investment philosophy.

With almost perfect timing, Brandes received a call one day from the brokerage receptionist asking if he could assist a walk-in customer with a stock purchase. As a rookie broker, he was responsible for all off-the-street business, which generally entails a lot of administrative work with little compensation in return. Much to his surprise, the customer standing in the lobby with no broker was Benjamin Graham, who wanted Brandes to purchase 1,000 shares of National Presto. Graham explained that he had just finished the update of *The Intelligent Investor*. He had used National Presto as an example of a company that met his strict value criteria and, therefore, was a good purchase candidate. Graham owned no National Presto and felt it would be somewhat hypocritical if he did not own any of the featured value stock in his book. (At that time, Graham had few stock holdings.) Prior to the crash of 1969–70, he sold all his stock positions and invested a majority of his money in tax-free bonds. (Brandes recalls that Graham was concentrating his time, effort, and abilities in a few more diverse and important areas—music, travel, and beautiful women—not necessarily in that order!) Brandes remembered the purchase in detail: "I bought 1,000 shares of National Presto at $33 per share."

At the time, Graham was spending the winter months in La Jolla, California, and Brandes had the opportunity to meet and speak with him frequently. He was intrigued by Graham's disciplined and rational method of stock selection, called *value investing*, as set down with David Dodd in the classic investment volume, *Security Analysis*. Brandes explained, "Here was something more than blue smoke and mirrors, something a person could get his teeth into and a rational means of measuring the worth of a heretofore elusive commodity, the common stock." Brandes remembered, "The light bulb went off in my head. I finally had a strategy that made rational sense." Outlined in Brandes's book, *Value Investing Today*, Graham passed on a number of value and safety guidelines. They are, as quoted from Brandes's text:

A. Value criteria
1. The earnings yield should be at least twice the AAA bond yield.
2. The stock's price/earnings ratio should be less than 40 percent of its highest price/earnings ratio of the previous five years.

3. The stock's dividend yield should be at least two thirds of the AAA bond yield.

4. The stock's price should be no more than two thirds of the company's tangible book value per share.

5. The company should be selling in the market for no more than two thirds of its net current assets.

B. Safety criteria

1. A company should owe no more than its worth. Total debt should not exceed book value. In other words, the debt/equity ratio should be less than 1.0.

2. The current assets should be less than twice the net current assets.

3. Total debt should be less than twice net current assets.

4. Earnings growth should have been at least 7 percent per annum compounded over the previous decade.

5. As an indication of stability of earnings, there should have been no more than two annual earnings declines of 5 percent or more during the previous decade.

Only stocks that met at least one value and one safety criteria were considered true bargains.

In short-cutting Benjamin Graham's criteria, Brandes believes portfolio candidates' financial characteristics should fall within these four basic guidelines:

1. No losses within the past five years.

2. Total debt is less than total tangible equity.

3. Share price is below its intrinsic book value.

4. Earnings yield should be 1½ to 2 times the 20-year, AAA rated bond yields.

With his newly learned trade, Brandes left the brokerage firm in March 1974 to found his own firm, now named Brandes Investment Partners, Inc. From 1974 to 1984, he refined his craft, applying the Graham & Dodd discipline and starting with a small core of private clients under a limited partnership structure and a client capital base of $500,000. Along the way, he acquired the designation of chartered financial analyst and a small staff of converts, some drawn from other brokerage firms. Over the last 10 years, the reputation of Brandes Investment Partners, Inc. has grown along with its clientele. From a small firm with a handful of clients and $50 million under management in 1985, the firm has grown to over $750 million under management and several hundred clients. Brandes can point with satisfaction to a 10-year annual track record in its global (including U.S. stock) accounts of over 19 percent and in its international (excluding U.S. stock) accounts of approximately 24 percent.

Today Brandes Investment Partners, Inc. consists of eight portfolio managers plus an administrative and trading staff. Charles Brandes is chief investment officer and head of the investment committee. Rounding out the core of the investment committee are managing directors Glenn Carlson and Jeffrey Busby, both chartered financial analysts as well. Barry O'Neil, with over 20 years' experience in the financial industry, heads the client services department.

Charles Brandes is regularly featured in *The Wall Street Journal, Barron's, Money, Outstanding Investor Digest* and numerous other financial publications. His first book, *Value Investing Today,* was published by Dow Jones-Irwin in 1989, and his second book, coauthored by Glenn Carlson and focusing on international investing, will be published in 1993 by Business One Irwin.

II.   THE STRATEGY—APPLYING GRAHAM & DODD TO THE WORLD ABROAD

What has led to this success story? The disciplined application of a long-term strategy known variously as *value investing* or *Graham & Dodd* has propelled the firm. Several basic, simple ideas drive value investing. One is that value investors *buy the business, not the stock.* A targeted business is analyzed to determine its true worth, which enables a valuation to be placed on the individual stock shares. Then the exchange price is compared to the intrinsic value. If the exchange price is discounted enough, there is a good chance for profit for the patient investor. This is a significant idea and worth emphasizing: if a security can be bought cheaply enough, there is a decent chance for profit even though the company itself may not be outstanding, or even particularly well run.

The other very basic tenet of value investing is that in the normal course of a market cycle there will indeed be stocks selling below their intrinsic worth. This disparity occurs because the stock markets are irrational and inefficient, especially in the foreign market where individual securities fall quickly in and out of favor. They feed on greed and fear rather than factual data. They can be swept by fads as easily and quickly as a French fashion show.

On a given day there are excellent businesses which attract a great deal of attention (glamour girls), and there are excellent businesses which attract no attention at all (the wallflowers). The difference between a glamour girl and a wallflower may be simply the expertise of Madison Avenue—how well the stock, the industry, or the particular CEO has been marketed. In other words, the market price does not reflect much about the true worth of a security. However, this is generally true: popular stocks tend to be expensive and unpopular stocks tend to be cheap. Another truism is that in the course of time, the worm will turn, and both steeply discounted and highly inflated prices will tend to approach their intrinsic values.

A. Patience Is a Virtue

Value investors look for the wallflowers with the intention of holding them for a full business cycle. A full business cycle would be defined here as three to five years. A long-term outlook is a must for a value investor. The Brandes definition of an *investor* is someone who purchases a security with the intention of holding it for a full business cycle, while a *speculator* is someone who purchases a security based on anticipated market movement with the intention of turning it over in less than a full business cycle.

This contrasts with the earnings momentum style adhered to within international investment advisory firms. Glenn Carlson commented, "The reason why we find so many bargains overseas is that, in foreign countries, little attention is placed on the basic value of a company. Investment dollars chase rumor and earnings growth projections, causing extreme cases of overvaluation and undervaluation."

B.   A Disciplined Approach

Buy and sell points are established ahead of time. The analysis of the business will provide a fair value for the stock. The value investor then looks to see at what price the security is currently selling. He is looking for a significant discount. If he can purchase a dollar's worth of stock for 70 cents, he has reached his goal. The opposite side of the coin is the sell point. When the discounted stock has climbed to its fair value level, it will be sold.

Buy and sell points are continually reevaluated by the investment committee to verify their validity. By establishing these dynamic points before the security is purchased and constantly updating them, the value investor has removed much of the emotion from the process and has reduced the risk of a steep price decline.

C.   Margin of Safety

A term frequently mentioned in the process is *margin of safety*. This is the difference between the intrinsic value of the stock and the price at which it is selling. As Glenn Carlson stated, "We make an estimate of what a company is worth and restrict our purchases to those companies selling at two thirds of their intrinsic value."

Consistent with this long-term philosophy, Brandes manages three quarters of a billion dollars with *no* stock quote machine in the firm's offices. Busby explained,

> With the second-by-second stock quotes, we'd take a short-term mentality that runs exactly counter to our long-term investment philosophy. Yes, we look at the daily newspapers, but given sufficient time, a diversified portfolio of undervalued stocks will produce. When someone buys a piece of real estate, they do not look to turn over the property tomorrow or next week or next month. Rather, they expect to hold it for several years. We are applying the same long-term principle to the stock market.

As long as the price is discounted below the value of the stock, the risk that the price will further decline significantly is lessened. When the price has risen to the intrinsic value (approximately 90 percent of Brandes's calculated net worth), there is no longer a margin of safety, and this is the point at which the stock will be sold. In Brandes's book, an excellent analogy is used to describe

EXHIBIT 4–1
Changes in World Equity Market

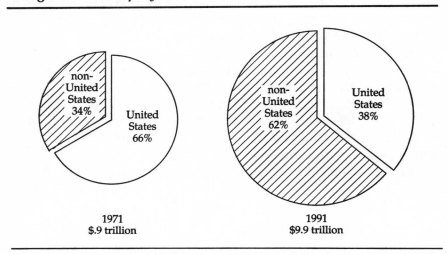

the margin of safety concept: "It is like going to the beach for a picnic . . . . You put your basket well back of the waterline. That distance between the basket and where the waves stop is your margin of safety."

Occasionally it happens that something significantly affects the security so that the intrinsic value itself drops. If the value drops to the price, the security will also be sold.

D.   Global Graham

The basic principles of Graham & Dodd are fairly well-known—the search for the low price/earnings ratio, low debt, high dividend yield, low price/book value, and low price/cash flow. What Brandes has done has been to make a very significant modification to an old, established discipline—he's shifted his orientation to the overseas markets.

When Benjamin Graham and David Dodd wrote *Security Analysis* back in the 1930s, the American stock market was the most significant equity arena worldwide. Consequently, value investing was applied only to the American market. As late as 1971, non-U.S. equity markets only amounted to 34 percent of the

EXHIBIT 4–2
Missed Opportunities

Domestic portfolios today miss investment opportunities in

7		insurance	
8		chemical	
8	of world's 10 largest	electronics	companies
8		automobile	
9		machinery	
9		utility	

Source: Center for International Financial Analysis & Research, Inc.

world's markets and totaled about $0.9 trillion (Exhibit 4–1). By 1991, the decimal had taken a startling move to the right. During those 20 years, the global share of non-U.S. markets had risen to $9.9 trillion, or 62 percent of the world equity market.

As highlighted in Exhibit 4–2, the investor who limits himself to only American issues effectively cuts himself off from two thirds of available opportunities and limits himself to a smaller performance playing field as well. Seventy-one out of 90 of the largest companies in nine industries are *not* American.

From 1980 to 1991, the best performance was abroad and from widely scattered regions. Italy, Australia, Norway, Hong Kong, and Mexico all took turns topping the list of star performers. Some markets experienced eye-popping increases. Austria, for example, was up 177 percent in 1986, Mexico 138 percent in 1991, and Korea 121 percent in 1988. During the same period of time, the best the United States could manage was a second place showing—only once. Exhibit 4–3 shows the rankings of the top five national stock markets each year since 1983. Note the highest finish of the U.S. market was fourth place in 1991, which wouldn't have even won show money at a horse race.

The disparity in performance between the U.S. and some foreign markets should not be surprising since many foreign economies are still expanding and emerging, in contrast to the more mature and stable U.S. market.

EXHIBIT 4–3
1983–1992 Stock Market Rankings

	1983	1984	1985	1986	1987
1st	Norway	Hong Kong	Austria	Spain	South Africa
2nd	Denmark	Spain	Germany	Italy	Japan
3rd	Australia	Japan	Italy	Japan	Spain
4th	Sweden	Belgium	Switzerland	Belgium	U.K.
5th	Netherlands	Netherlands	France	France	Canada

	1988	1989	1990	1991	1992 YTD
1st	Belgium	Thailand	Netherlands	Philippines	Philippines
2nd	Denmark	Austria	Italy	Hong Kong	Hong Kong
3rd	Sweden	Philippines	U.K.	Australia	Switzerland
4th	Norway	South Africa	Hong Kong	U.S.	France
5th	Thailand	Germany	Austria	Singapore	Germany

Source: Morgan Stanley Capital International.

The principles of value investing can be applied to any business. Brandes had the necessary insight to pursue this strategy to the next level—beyond political boundaries. As a consequence, Brandes Investment Partners, Inc. has been purchasing foreign securities for its clients' portfolios for almost 20 years.

There are definite benefits to the investor who will venture abroad. The obvious one is that he has a greater universe of opportunities from which to choose. Sound companies can be found anywhere in the world and, in this age of global conglomerates, the home office may not be where you expect it. In other words, a business is a business no matter where it is located.

More than that, some of the largest corporations in existence are located beyond U.S. borders. The distinction between U.S. and foreign companies is becoming blurred. Buy a Ford lately? The transmission may have been built in Japan, and assembly may have taken place in Mexico.

Some familiar names which we consider as American as apple pie are actually based abroad. Lipton ice tea, Nestlé chocolate, and even Burger King are all foreign-owned. Shockingly, the Pillsbury dough boy has a British accent!

Increasingly, U.S. corporations look overseas for sales. Many U.S. companies have more sales overseas than here in the U.S., and more and more jobs in American companies are being moved offshore. There is an opposing trend as well, as foreign companies are employing more people here in the states, and sometimes the American market is larger than the home market. Clearly, provincial "buy American" thinking is outdated in terms of investing in businesses.

The typical U.S. consumer spends 25 to 30 percent on foreign-made or foreign-owned goods. Therefore, the overseas investor participates in the profits of the businesses which are selling their products and services over here. The investor who holds Volkswagen, for example, owns a piece of a company which has a major market right here in the U.S. If the prices on German goods become inflated, that investor is hedged against the effects simply through his ownership of stock.

E. Independent World Markets

Another advantage of foreign investment is perhaps less obvious: diversification. A prudent investor will spread his investable funds among a number of securities. Being able to diversify among countries, as well, adds yet another layer of protection as demonstrated in the risk return analysis in Exhibit 4–4.

We tend to think of markets in the "us versus them" manner (U.S. as opposed to everybody else): a significant, positive point. The U.S. market moves differently from overseas markets, and lackluster performance on Wall Street may be offset by good performance elsewhere.

In fact, markets in individual countries are separate entities, and all tend to operate independently from one another. News which will cause the Norwegian market to plummet may not cause so much as a ripple on the Hong Kong pond. This is good news for the investor with stocks in widely diversified markets, for the volatility of his portfolio is greatly reduced.

Historically, the benefits to a U.S.-based investor who committed a portion of his assets overseas have been clear. As presented in Exhibit 4–5, an overseas element has been shown to significantly increase returns while reducing the risk of the overall portfolio.

EXHIBIT 4–4
Risk Return Analysis (3 *Years Ending December 31, 1991*)

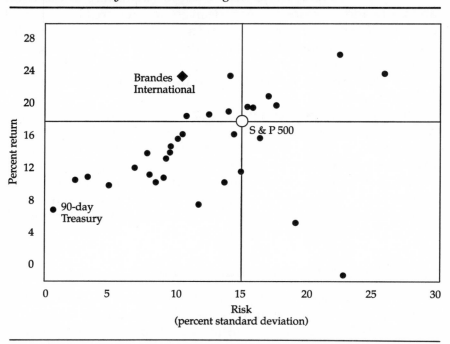

F.   The Investment Process

Detailed analysis is the key to uncovering value opportunities. Potential securities are examined by Brandes's investment committee. A global universe will include approximately 8,000 securities. Brandes makes use of a wide range of vehicles to screen for potential candidates—computer databases, global periodicals, research analysts, company reports, even visits to foreign sites. This screening is followed by in-depth, bottom-up analysis. Fundamentals of a company, such as its asset values, earnings, cash flows, return on invested capital, and subsidiaries, are all analyzed. Busby explained, "We don't need to know what a company is worth down to the last paper clip; rather, just a general net worth calculation will suffice."

EXHIBIT 4–5
Global Diversification Advantages (1985–1991)

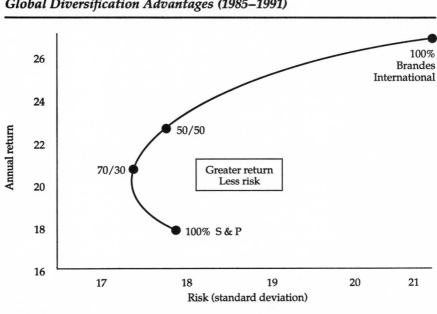

All research is conducted in-house on publicly available information. There is no reliance on market models or forecasts, no
matter how expert the forecaster—only on factual, measurable
data.

Securities are purchased if they meet value criteria—that is,
absolute low price/book, price/cash flow, price/earnings, and
debt/equity ratios with consistent earnings and attractive yields.
In Benjamin Graham's book, *Security Analysis,* he advocated the
purchase of a stock that met the strict criteria of selling at less than
two thirds of a company's net current assets. (*Net current assets*
means cash and equivalents on hand, including immediate salable
inventory, minus all liabilities, including off-balance sheet liabilities such as capital leases or unfunded pension liabilities. Fixed
and intangible assets are purchased for less than nothing since
you're buying liquid assets at a discount. Nothing is paid for
intangible assets, such as goodwill.)

Today, both in the U.S. and global markets, no good companies are selling at these cheap levels; therefore, the criteria are relaxed so that the least expensive companies in the world are considered by Brandes for purchase. For example, Graham suggested the purchase of companies with earnings yields of two times long-term, AAA-rated government bonds. Brandes has adjusted this benchmark to one and a half times the bond yield. Also, instead of purchasing stocks at five times earnings, Brandes will stretch the criteria to eight to ten times earnings. In other words, the lowest trench/best value stocks are the candidates for purchase.

Once the value screens have identified the cheap companies, Brandes goes directly to the company for specific information and reports *and* analyzes Wall Street research reports on the specific companies to determine whether or not something has been missed. Brandes and his team ask, "Is there some major, insurmountable cause for this company's mispricing?"

A portfolio will be allocated among 20 to 30 issues. Typically, no more than 5 percent will be committed to a single security, nor more than 20 percent to a particular industry or foreign country. No attempt is made to match any index allocations, just to find the best value. Brandes Investment Partners's largest 10 holdings as of December 31, 1991, were:

China Light & Power ADR.
Hong Kong Shanghai Bank ADR.
Hanson PLC ADR.
Salomon Inc.
Sandoz Registered Shares ADR.
Jardine Matheson Hldg ADR.
British Steel PLC ADR.
Telefonica De Espana SA ADS.
Liberty Bankcorp Inc.
Hutchison Whampoa ADR.

That means that a client may have no exposure to the hot market of the moment, since hot markets usually have inflated prices. It also means that a client may have no exposure to a large market if it is overvalued, despite its size. Japan is a good example. Brandes has not purchased a Japanese stock since 1986. (Brandes's clients have been very happy about its positioning as the Nikkei averages have been plunging.) On the other hand, for the past two years, the Hong Kong market has represented the best value with the 1997 Chinese political overhangings. Brandes has maintained almost 20 percent exposure to this market wrought with what he calls "screaming values."

The investment stance in an account at a given time will be determined by the number of attractive equity opportunities versus the issues which have been sold after becoming fairly valued. This balance dictates the level of cash reserves.

Brandes does not hedge against foreign currency exchange rate fluctuations since a long-term time horizon and uncertain holding period make hedging look very unattractive economically. In addition, hedging is of dubious value to someone looking overseas for the diversification benefits.

In the final analysis, 75 percent of the analysis is financial statement–related, and 25 percent is based on subjective judgments of the Brandes investment committee. According to Brandes,

> Before purchasing a stock, we want to read, think, and talk about the company. We are in no hurry. Before purchase, we want to have an understanding of the company and the nature of its business and industry. This use of quality, subjective judgment distinguishes Brandes from Graham & Dodd analysis, where only balance sheet numbers matter.

G. The Market Timing Myths and Quarterly Earning Projection

It should be apparent by now that value investors deal with the market as is, not the way they hope it will be. Analysis is of clearly measurable data. There is no attempt to anticipate the direction of short-term market moves as market timers do.

The concept of market timing is based on the idea that the market sends certain signals when it is about to change directions and that an astute investor can interpret these signals and react accordingly. When the market signals decline, a move is made to get out of equities, and, conversely, when the market appears to be heating up, the move is back into equities. It is a great theory, but it does not work consistently.

In October 1987, many prices fell steeply. Experts had been predicting the market's collapse for months and, of course, eventually prices did adjust. However, there were as many opinions as to the severity of the correction and the duration as experts available, and the predictions ranged from "a depressed market for a short term" to "a disaster lasting for years."

Clearly, if market forecasts were as effective as their proponents claim, the predictions from the same data would not have ranged so widely. The market is simply not so accommodating as to send unambiguous signals. Too many factors act at once. While chemicals, for example, are flashing warning signs, industrials may be healthy. The market timer is then faced with the dilemma of which signal to react to: shall I stay or shall I go?

In addition, Brandes cares little about quarter-to-quarter earnings changes. Analysts determine how a specific company calculates its earnings, but no attempt is made to forecast the earnings. This important point distinguishes Brandes from growth managers whose style depends on the accurate projection of earnings.

The value investor is relieved to be able to forgo the stress of trying to decipher the market's vagaries and to fall back on value criteria, which will enable him to select securities in all types of markets. The only form of technical analysis Brandes uses is the monitoring and ranking of the worst performing markets in the world because it is in these markets that one finds the bargain values.

H. Preservation of Capital in Declining Markets

During periods of price declines, value-oriented portfolios show a better ability to preserve capital. As shown in Exhibits 4–6 and 4–7, Brandes's strict value disciplines have protected its clients' net worth during market declines, yet provided competitive returns during up market cycles. The likelihood of major price drops is reduced since securities have been bought at a discount in the first place. That is not to say that there might not be some deterioration in the price (after all, these will often be unpopular issues), but the chance that the decline will be major or permanent is lessened.

EXHIBIT 4–6
Yearly Percentage Return in Up and Down Markets

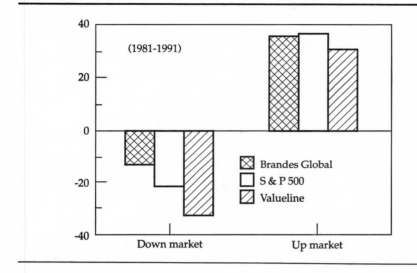

Value investors have another ace in the hole in declining markets. They are able to buy more issues when prices go down and therefore are better positioned to take advantage of the next price increase whenever it occurs. By the time the market timers have enough data collected to be able to determine it is time to get back in the market, sizable increases may have already passed them by.

I.   Efficient Market Theory Myth

Hand-in-hand with market timing goes the myth that the price of each security is based on factual data and reflects the actual worth of the issue. Proponents argue that with rapid communications, all knowable data is accounted for, and therefore, no undervalued securities exist. Value investors have smiled and proved them wrong for over 60 years now.

Any rational observer can see fads sweep through the markets as investors are sold on the idea that a particular security is the next IBM. When optic fibers came out, for example, they were what everyone had to have. A new advance in medical science will swell the ranks of investors in that field.

EXHIBIT 4–7
Yearly Percentage Return in Up and Down Markets

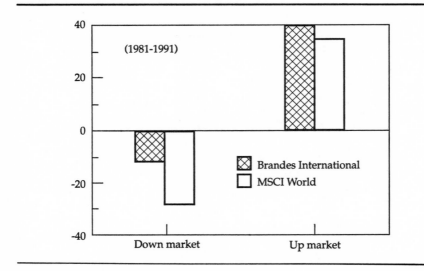

Crowd-following creates a ripple effect as perfectly good securities are jettisoned from accounts in order to make room for the new darling. Another effect of following the crowd is that prices for that issue begin to rise, and the late jumpers-on-the-bandwagon have to pay more and more. That does not mean that the security is worth more. The value of the security is the same: the quoted price has just been driven up by demand. There is no efficiency in the price of a popular security.

Conversely, the price of an unpopular security may be depressed by lack of interest. There is no efficiency in this price either, but joy for the value investor because that is exactly what he is looking for. In discussing the efficient market hypothesis, Brandes stated,

> The global market and related specific stock prices are manic and have nothing to do with the real value of a company. How can a company be worth 50 percent or less [based on the market value] from one year to the next when the fundamentals, or basic value, have changed only slightly? History shows us time and time again that the value is there. It's just that the markets are inappropriately pricing the security.

J.   A Secret Fishing Hole

Just as an angler may have a special place no one else knows about where he can always be sure of a catch, a value investor has something extra going for him: value investing is a contrarian approach which goes against the mainstream. That is the case in the U.S. and even more so abroad. U.S.-based managers who look beyond U.S. borders use almost exclusively a top-down approach. They try to forecast broad, macroeconomic factors which they use to determine country weightings, in effect betting on countries and markets. They pay a great deal of attention to indexes, particularly the Morgan Stanley EAFE index (Europe, Australia, and the Far East). The end result of this investment process is a decision to over- or underweight countries or regions. The business itself, as represented by the security, receives the least attention. Very few in this country are looking for discounted overseas securities.

Not only are the U.S.-based investors not using the principles of value investing, but foreign investors are not using them either. Foreign investors tend to be earnings- and earnings momentum–oriented. Expectations of poor earnings may be enough to crush the market price of an issue, and little or nothing halts the drop once started. Few pools of capital are available which are deliberately seeking depressed issues and will start to snap them up, as in this country. The end result is little competition abroad for bargains—Brandes has had the fishing hole to himself. As a consequence, Brandes's international accounts have outperformed the Morgan Stanley EAFE index by a startling 20 percent annual differential for the five years ended March 31, 1992.

III.   A FINAL WORD

Value investing has a 60-year track record of providing very satisfactory returns for patient investors. It is a disciplined approach which enables its practitioners to participate in all but the most inflated markets and to acquire solid issues at reasonable prices.

In the five years prior to 1992, value investing has lagged as the broad market emerges. If the first two quarters of 1992 are any indication, this trend seems to be reversing itself. But value investing is more than a short-term phenomenon. A look at the top-rated investment managers over the past 25 years shows a few well-known advisers consistently make the list: Warren Buffett, Pacific Partners, Stan Perimeter, Sequoia Fund, Walter Shloss, Tweedy Browne, and Charles Munger. Each follows its own slight variation and version of Benjamin Graham's value analysis.

Brandes Investment Partners, Inc. has moved this classic strategy up to the next level by advancing into the global arena. Value investors who look worldwide triple their field of opportunities. As Carlson stated, "Seventy percent of the investment opportunities lie outside of the U.S. market. We believe that not only better values can be found overseas, but that clients' performance will reflect our worldwide bargain shopping." Looking ahead, Brandes added, "Foreign economies have the potential to grow much faster than that of the U.S. Also, the world is a much more positive place. Governments are becoming more free market–oriented, interest rates and barriers to entry are down, and privatization of business is on the rise." He waxed philosophically, "All the wealth in the world is generated by private businesses. Real estate, bonds, gold, or oil are not wealth; they are expenses to a business. We concentrate our efforts in buying businesses, not expenses, where the real wealth is created."

Brandes uses a rational process which focuses on tangible data to analyze and determine intrinsic worth. Then only the most attractive issues are selected from this expanded and well-stocked pool. The Brandes approach is designed for investors who seek long-term, worldwide capital appreciation, along with diversification and conservative management. Brandes offers a thoughtful, disciplined approach to the international markets. If you are the kind of investor that likes securities selling at steep discounts, plus have the vision to encompass a global marketplace and the patience to wait for other investors to recognize this value, Brandes Investment Partners, Inc. may be just the manager for you. Brandes is perfect for those of you who have the psychological make-up to detach yourselves from the day-to-day market fluctuations. Value investing regulates a contrarian mind-set and demands the willingness to purchase what others perceive as distasteful securities trading in unpopular and unloved markets.

Conceptually, we understand the merits of this approach. But in reality, it is a difficult strategy to put into practice. As Brandes's impressive track record indicates, the best opportunities for capital growth and profits fall within areas which require investor vision and strong stomachs.

Chapter Five

Roger Engemann & Associates

"Remember my son, that any man who is a bear on the future of this country will go broke."

J. P. Morgan, 1908

I. THE COOL BULLS

Inscribed on Roger Engemann's tombstone will be "This is the guy who believed in common stocks." As one of America's foremost preachers of growth stock investing, Engemann allows no stock market pessimism to pervade his mind: "Optimism wins—it is a basic fact of life." Spreading his gospel, Roger Engemann and his associates (REA) believe that growth common stocks provide the best avenue for achieving financial goals such as putting children through college and providing for a comfortable retirement.

To justify that recommendation, the team likes to point to a favorite graph prominently displayed in many offices at REA: the wealth indices chart, published by Ibbotson Associates in Chicago (see Chapter 1). The chart presents a compelling case for equities when compared over the long term to two alternative investments: Treasury bills and long-term government bonds. A dollar invested in Treasury bills in 1925 grew to $11.40 by the end of 1992, for an annual compounded rate of return of 3.70 percent. The same investment in long-term government bonds grew to $23.71, for a 4.84 percent growth rate. However, the same dollar invested in common stocks grew to $727.38, for an average annual return of 10.34 percent. Put simply, an investment in common stocks would be worth more than 30 times as much as either of the other two.

REA has created an almost utopian work environment which looks out over a patio and lovely garden overflowing with brightly colored flowers—a picture of tranquility and peace. In discussing REA's work setting, Engemann commented, "I deliberately created a calm environment in which we can effectively make decisions. Unless you have a positive view toward the world and common stocks, you might as well give it up and hide your cash in a tin can in your backyard." Roy Ishii, chief financial and operating officer, stated, "This place is like Disneyland. I don't mean to imply that it is frivolous. But it is a very pleasant place to work."

Today, REA employs over 130 people and maintains an office in Greenwich, Connecticut, as well as its headquarters in Pasadena, California. The firm is 100 percent owned by its active employees. Over 20 key employees have ownership, plus REA provides a liberally funded pension and ESOP plan. Assets under management totaled $4.9 billion as of December 31, 1992, most of which are in individually managed common stock portfolios with a minimum account size of $100,000. Approximately $800 million is in the Pasadena group of mutual funds, a family of three funds managed by a subsidiary, Roger Engemann Management Company, Inc. Putting his own money on the line, Roger is a large investor in the Pasadena funds.

II.   HISTORY AND INVESTMENT PHILOSOPHY—UNWAVERING OPTIMISM

Where did Roger Engemann's perpetual optimism come from? He grew up very poor, but even at a young age he believed that life would somehow be good to him. While many children in his situation ended up in unemployment lines or lower-paid blue collar positions, Engemann attended the University of Oregon and then pursued graduate studies in economics at UCLA.

In the mid-1960s, Engemann, freshly armed with a master's degree in economics, set out to find a job. Fortunately for the investing public, no jobs were available in economics, and he accepted a position as a money manager for the Bank of America. After just three years of experience there and in a brokerage research department, he started his own firm at the ripe age of 29. With only $4 million in assets, he hooked up with a business manager of entertainment celebrities and arranged to manage the celebrities' assets. Commenting on those lean times, Engemann glibly stated, "it [the management fee] did not pay enough to live on, but neither did my bank salary."

Although his stint at the Bank of America was short, Engemann credits the investment philosophy of the firm's then chief investment officer, Al Golding, with having a significant influence on the development of his own growth stock theory. Golding, who retired early from the bank via his own personal investment success, taught Engemann that the ideal company is one in which both the earnings and price/earnings multiple are growing rapidly. He believed that a stock will always produce for a portfolio as long as the earnings are growing.

The other person who heavily influenced Engemann was Mike Mork, his first employee, who now runs his own successful investment firm, Mork Capital, located 150 miles north of San Francisco. Engemann recounted, "Mike had a burning desire to follow the growth stock approach." He feels blessed with the opportunity to have worked with those two key individuals early in his career.

REA's portfolio managers look for core companies—those which continue to meet expectations year in and year out. In describing his favorite portfolio holding of all time, Engemann threw out this statistic: "Had you invested $1,650 for 100 shares of Wal-Mart in 1970, today your holding would be worth over $4 million." Rejecting the value philosophy made famous by Benjamin Graham, Engemann commented, "I've studied how one can buy value stocks at bargain levels, but these type of companies make me uncomfortable. There is some reason behind their bargain prices. These companies have continued to underperform or failed or been rejected. In addition, they have a knack for disappointing you. In other words, these bargain value companies are not fun to own!"

Assets did not grow like weeds for Roger Engemann. In fact, they grew very slowly for the first five to six years. In addition, he had to cope with an unnerving and volatile market. The original $4 million grew to over $27 million by 1973 (with 1973 being his second best performance year), but declined sharply back to $5 million during the devastating 1974 bear market. Even during the darkest days when clients were heading for the exit door and portfolio capital values were eroding, Engemann never lost faith in either himself or his investment philosophy.

Looking back to those painful times, he commented, "Any client who stuck with me through 1974 has never left." He continued with a philosophical tone: "I've seen both fabulous and horrible times; therefore, the market movements do not bother me. You can read all the books you want, but until you've been pummeled by the market, you will not learn how to handle stress and management of client funds." The year 1974 signaled the bottom for REA. In 1977, with only $17 million under management, business began to grow, and by 1980, its client asset base had risen to $40 million. During the next four years, assets under management more than quadrupled to over $164 million.

From the beginning, REA concentrated its effort in attracting and cultivating individual portfolios in the $100,000 to $1,000,000 size. In describing this target market, Engemann stated, "We have always gained a high satisfaction level and long-term relationships in assisting individuals build wealth." As an example of the significance of these long-term relationships, Engemann pulled out a statement showing an existing client's inception and quarterly values starting in 1973 and continuing through the end of 1992 (Exhibit 5–1). Clearly, the client has weathered three rough periods (the first two years—1973–74; the stock market crash of 1987; and Iraq's invasion of Kuwait in 1990). Citing the client's patience, Engemann stated, "He survived through these severe downdrafts and found that his portfolio rebounded sharply after each decline."

As page 3 of Exhibit 5–1 indicates, the client invested a total of $224,392, and has seen his capital grow over *29 times* his net contributions while under REA portfolio supervision. This is compared to approximately an eightfold increase in the S&P 500 and

EXHIBIT 5–1
Actual Account Performance Report

Date	Account no.: 182603 Amount Added or (Withdrawn)	Value of Account	Account name: sample individual Account with Income	S&P Inc.	DJ Inc.
04/22/93					
03/17/73	50,000.00	50,000.00	100.00	100.00	100.00
03/31/73		49,929.05	99.86	98.33	98.88
06/30/73		45,660.94	91.32	92.65	93.58
09/30/73		58,459.38	116.92	97.09	100.29
12/31/73		52,597.73	105.20	88.13	91.05
03/31/74		48,991.88	97.98	85.71	91.58
06/30/74		46,475.26	92.95	79.26	87.79
09/30/74		41,055.65	82.11	59.41	67.53
12/31/74		42,204.61	84.41	64.92	69.46
03/31/75	10,000.00	61,999.85	104.00	79.80	87.64
06/30/75	15,000.00	91,201.24	127.82	92.01	101.38
09/30/75		78,052.05	109.39	82.00	92.66
12/31/75		86,808.38	121.66	89.06	100.55
03/31/76		107,429.58	150.57	102.40	118.98
06/30/76		96,821.18	135.70	104.86	120.50
09/30/76		96,769.82	135.63	106.83	120.15
12/31/76		110,295.68	154.58	110.16	123.20
03/31/77	25,000.00	130,201.54	148.20	102.05	114.03
06/30/77		136,667.66	155.56	105.38	115.03
09/30/77		140,345.20	159.75	102.49	107.77
12/31/77		155,585.64	177.10	102.26	107.23
03/31/78		158,647.96	180.58	97.33	99.30
06/30/78		178,590.71	203.28	105.56	108.83
09/30/78		203,341.55	231.46	114.70	116.58
12/31/78		191,384.38	217.85	109.04	110.09
03/31/79		198,307.36	225.73	116.82	119.63
06/30/79		200,885.14	228.66	119.97	118.54
09/30/79		215,502.00	245.30	129.12	125.44
12/31/79	25,000.00	245,809.90	250.90	129.29	121.63
03/31/80		233,838.14	238.68	123.93	115.75
06/30/80		254,843.88	260.12	140.47	129.78
09/30/80	100,000.00	416,373.85	317.99	156.06	141.41
12/31/80		455,700.91	348.03	170.83	148.28
03/31/81		497,942.34	380.29	173.21	156.54
06/30/81		527,637.81	402.97	169.27	154.48
09/30/81		463,086.11	353.67	151.99	136.62
12/31/81		523,838.63	400.07	162.54	142.88
03/31/82	50,000.00	541,121.58	374.83	150.86	136.67

EXHIBIT 5–1
(continued)

Date	Account no.: 182603 Amount Added or (Withdrawn)	Account name: sample individual Value of Account	Account with Income	S&P Inc.	DJ Inc.
06/30/82		567,430.48	393.06	149.97	137.08
09/30/82		635,990.21	440.55	167.19	153.67
12/31/82	50,000.00	886,066.17	574.91	197.64	181.71
03/31/83	100,000.00	1,119,965.49	654.93	217.35	198.54
06/30/83		1,246,377.12	728.85	241.32	217.03
09/30/83		1,218,077.38	712.30	240.94	221.51
12/31/83		1,195,885.30	699.33	241.78	228.60
03/31/84		1,123,318.98	656.89	235.93	214.16
06/30/84	320,000.00−	824,820.58	669.46	229.69	210.75
09/30/84		886,298.48	719.36	251.97	227.50
12/31/84		876,186.33	711.16	256.59	231.26
03/31/85		993,033.69	805.99	280.01	244.59
06/30/85		1,074,274.88	871.93	300.42	260.84
09/30/85		988,399.78	802.23	288.23	262.53
12/31/85		1,187,698.78	963.99	337.65	308.79
03/31/86		1,397,958.90	1134.65	384.96	366.46
06/30/86	119,392.00	1,708,251.45	1282.97	407.51	384.76
09/30/86		1,487,785.68	1117.39	379.17	362.81
12/31/86		1,564,889.23	1175.30	400.17	392.60
03/31/87		1,936,813.69	1454.63	485.19	480.54
06/30/87		1,893,610.95	1422.18	509.30	507.87
09/30/87		1,937,032.90	1454.79	542.81	548.74
12/31/87		1,626,103.30	1221.27	420.96	413.95
03/31/88		1,696,787.71	1274.36	444.96	428.11
06/30/88		1,759,223.66	1321.25	474.25	465.18
09/30/88		1,768,123.87	1327.94	475.95	463.18
12/31/88		1,788,727.91	1343.41	490.58	479.77
03/31/89		1,953,570.42	1467.21	525.45	511.87
06/30/89		2,155,068.52	1618.55	571.48	549.25
09/30/89		2,436,578.41	1829.97	632.49	611.36
12/31/89		2,441,027.12	1833.31	645.30	631.20
03/31/90		2,409,720.45	1809.80	626.20	627.03
06/30/90		2,805,907.20	2107.35	665.10	673.64
09/30/90		2,096,436.68	1574.51	574.22	579.65
12/31/90		2,413,233.12	1812.44	625.47	628.68
03/31/91		3,050,531.73	2291.08	716.41	701.50
06/30/91		3,014,330.25	2263.89	714.37	705.42
09/30/91		3,416,360.35	2565.83	752.29	737.68

04/22/93

EXHIBIT 5–1
(continued)

Date	Account no.: 182603 Amount Added or (Withdrawn)	Value of Account	Account name: sample individual Account with Income	S&P Inc.	DJ Inc.
12/31/91		3,935,947.94	2956.06	815.14	780.72
03/31/92		3,768,102.12	2830.00	794.93	802.77
06/30/92		3,536,667.58	2656.19	809.70	829.42
09/30/92		3,675,483.18	2760.44	835.07	824.23
12/31/92		3,921,002.69	2944.84	877.26	838.26
NET ADDITIONS	224,392.00				

SAMPLE INDIVIDUAL

held at The Bank of
California

December 31, 1992   STATEMENT OF ASSETS   ACCT. 182603

Summary of Portfolio

	Cost or Other Basis	Market Value	Percent of Account	Estimated Annual Income	Current Yield
Common stocks	1,928,081.53	3,838,668.75	97.90	55,567.00	1.45
Accrued income	4,163.00	4,163.00	.11	.00	.00
Cash and equivalents	78,170.94	78,170.94	1.99	2,001.18	2.56
Total account	2,010,415.47	3,921,002.69		57,568.18	1.47

This performance report and statement of assets are distributed with the permission of our client to illustrate the form and contents of these reports, which reflect the actual performance results and the current portfolio composition of an existing account employing an unrestricted investment strategy. While most of the returns resulted from capital appreciation, these figures include the reinvestment of all income and are after the payment of investment counseling fees, brokerage commissions, and custodian fees. Figures for the Standard & Poor's 500 and the Dow Jones Industrial Average include the reinvestment of dividends. As you review this information, please keep in mind that the past results offer no guarantee of future performance.

B R O A D W A Y

D E L I

PATRICIA COLIN
DELI CATERING MANAGER

1457 3RD STREET PROMENADE
SANTA MONICA, CA 90401
310-451-8708
Fax: 310-451-0537

EDGAR

the Dow Jones Industrial Average. The results of other clients are similar to Exhibit 5–1, as clients own many of the same basic securities. Put another way, a $100,000 investment in 1970 would have increased to over $4 million—almost four times the capital increase of the S&P 500.

III.   STRATEGY—THE GROWTH STOCK PROSPECTORS—TURNING OVER STONES LOOKING FOR A FEW GOLD NUGGETS

Since Mike Mork's departure in 1984, his shoes have been adeptly filled by REA's two key portfolio managers/senior analysts, Jim Mair and John Tilson, with Janice Keyser handling day-to-day portfolio administration. Mair and Tilson are the two people who determine the asset allocation and stock selection. In other words, they "pull the trigger" for both the individual and mutual fund portfolios. Prior to hitching up with REA, Mair and Tilson managed money with bank trust departments, brokerage firms, and insurance companies. Both knew Engemann well before joining his firm, and when the opportunity arose for them to join REA, they knew their employment would be a good fit. Together they have overseen REA's rapid growth from $164 million in 1984 to over $4.9 billion at the end of 1992.

In describing portfolio strategy, Tilson bluntly stated, "People try to make this business overly complicated. Our strategy is simple—we find good businesses, buy into them, and then hold them until they quit growing. This is not rocket scientist stuff." What separates these two stockpickers from unsuccessful investors are three important attributes:

1. The ability and skills to identify those stable but fast-growing companies.
2. The skill to identify and distinguish the important and relevant information about a company. In other words, being able to separate the facts from the noise.
3. The temperament and confidence to stay with or buy into positions/companies when everyone else is heading for the exit doors.

Trying to pin down their specific stock selecting rules is like trying to pin down a spot of mercury on a flat table. The reason: Mair and Tilson do not have, nor do they believe in, any rigid investment rules. They are convinced that complex decision-making structures impede performance. Mair flatly stated, "The more screens or filters you have, the poorer investment decision you'll make; with each filter some valuable information is lost."

Beginning with the asset allocation strategy, REA's portfolio managers do not believe in market timing or technical analysis. The only broad, economic statistics they analyze are monetary policy, interest rates, supplier deliveries, and inflation. Using Engemann's expertise as a trained economist, they are particularly interested in the trends of those economic statistics. On a longer-term basis, savings rates are also monitored. Engemann commented, "The higher the savings rate in America, the more capital available for economic growth." Regarding inflation, Engemann described his philosophy by paraphrasing Will Rogers: "I'm not for *in*flation or *de*flation—just flation."

Mair and Tilson normally keep client portfolios fully invested. Mid-1987 was the last time REA sold positions because of economic conditions. The only other occasions when stock values became excessive, and therefore were sold, were in 1974 and 1979. Otherwise, it maintains a 90–98 percent invested position in its core, favorite portfolio holdings. The economic conditions giving rise to the sale of stocks are rising interest rates, inflation, and stock prices. This mixture can be highly combustible and usually leads to a bear market in stocks.

REA's portfolio selection strategy begins with an analysis of those companies which it believes will grow at and sustain a 15 to 20 percent gain per year. This master list of stocks, which hovers around 100 in size, was put together over the years, one stock at a time. There is not a computer model where all the variables are entered and "flash"—a list of buy candidates are listed. Again, REA is looking for a comfort level in its stock holdings—stocks that will produce earnings growth year after year. As Tilson stated, "The average earnings growth rate of companies in America runs at 7 percent per year, so we are looking for those companies that can earn two to three times the average."

Because of this strong desire for comfort, REA is especially attuned to monopoly or near monopoly situations such as Coca-Cola and Philip Morris. Today, with "brand demand" becoming a worldwide phenomenon, companies with franchise-like dominance are showing significant gains in the global marketplace. Take a franchise stock like Philip Morris as an example. Not only are earnings growing at 15 to 20 percent per year, but the U.S. government has forbidden the use of TV cigarette advertising, which in effect removes all newcomers to the business. Engemann stated, "It is impossible for a company to 'rise out of the ashes' to compete on a long-term basis against Philip Morris." Typically, REA avoids commodity-driven industries such as oil and precious metals. Companies in these businesses tend to respond to short-term supply/demand conditions in their own unique ways rather than in a consistent, predictable pattern.

Describing the types of companies REA invests in reminds one of a college Psychology 101 class where Maslow's hierarchy of needs is detailed. Engemann laid out his simple philosophy:

> In a developing or third world country where a fellow is afraid of being eaten by a tiger and his standard of living begins to rise, he reaches out for a cigarette (à la Philip Morris). Then, he wants something sweet to drink, so he asks for a Coke. Cigarettes and Cokes are modest expenditures. As his standard of living continues to rise, he desires better medical care (Merck), followed by entertainment (Walt Disney, Toys "R" Us), consumer goods (Gillette, Wal-Mart), and finally, airplanes (Boeing).

It sounds overly simplistic, but an examination of the portfolio supports this philosophy.

What gives REA the confidence to buy and stay with its core holdings is its extensive use of visits to the companies to meet with executives. The search for companies is more than just a paper search. Mair and Tilson spend over 50 percent of their time in the field, conducting on-site visits with the management of companies being followed. As a result, their investment conclusions are based on direct, timely information. REA spends $1–2 million per year for research and travel to meet with representatives of their stock holdings. Before making a trip, portfolio managers read everything they can about the company, including quarterlies, annuals, and research reports. At the meeting, they attempt to analyze the condition of the company. Basic questions during the interview with management include:

- Who are your competitors? What are they doing that concerns you? How are you responding to these competitive threats?
- Who are your customers? Who are your suppliers?
- How many stores are you going to build?
- How are you going to undersell your competitors?
- Are there any stock plans (repurchases or issues)?
- How do the gross margins look?

Then, REA portfolio managers go back six months or a year later to find out what transpired and continue the questions. By making visits year in and year out, REA builds a detailed file with which to track the company. It obtains better information because the firm works harder, not because it is smarter. Put simply, REA just spends a tremendous amount of time looking at the management of companies they find to be attractive.

Over the past 25 years, REA's portfolio managers have visited thousands of companies and built long-standing and close relationships with the managements of their portfolio holdings. In discussing this relationship, Engemann stated, "The managements of companies are highly ethical. Seldom are we misled or lied to. The reason is simple: Liars, in the long run, lose in this world. Sam Walton, deceased founder of Wal-Mart, is a perfect example. Wal-Mart, being one of REA's earliest and largest holdings, has provided crystal clear information." He continued, "If Sam Walton said the sky is blue, the sky is blue."

Periodically, economic conditions will cause the stock price to drop. REA, by knowing the company intimately, has the confidence to stay with it (or buy more stock) during these shaky times. Engemann commented, "Whenever I get a little nervous about the market, I jump out of my chair to visit the companies we own. After hearing the great things these managements are doing, that anxiousness quickly vanishes. Most investors recoil or hide when a solid, growing company's stock declines—we tend to be active buyers of the stock." Engemann seems to enjoy market declines because it gives his portfolio managers the opportunity to buy more of their favorite growth stocks. More importantly, the declines wash out the market's hot money. The market doesn't need that level of what Engemann calls the "fluff speculator."

Currently, REA's focus is on large companies selling at what it considers to be very reasonable prices. The 12 holdings that make up over 50 percent of its client asset base are:

Carnival Cruise Lines, Inc.	The Gillette Company.	Federal Home Loan Mortgage Corporation (Freddie Mac).
Circus Circus Enterprises.	NationsBank Corporation.	Pfizer, Inc.
Federal National Mortgage Association (Fannie Mae).	Philip Morris Companies Incorporated.	Wal-Mart Stores, Inc.
	Reuters Holdings PLC.	The Walt Disney Company.
	Toys "R" Us.	

REA's primary interest is not the price paid for a particular stock. Tilson stated,

> If a company grows at 15 to 20 percent per year, you can and should be willing to pay a higher price (based on its price/earnings multiple). On the other hand, if a company is growing at 7 percent per year, the price you pay is everything. And that is the difference between a value and a growth manager. There are no hard and fast rules regarding the price you can pay for a growth stock. Take Circus Circus—we will pay a premium for a first-rate company like this because the earnings consistently meet or exceed our expectations.

Although REA is not adverse to using small stocks for the client and mutual fund portfolios, small companies run the risk of not providing consistent earnings (they are more likely to disappoint you, leading to sharp stock price declines). Engemann commented, "While the future of the world is dependent on the growth rate of small companies, the failure rate is high." There is also a tendency by REA to use American companies because of the comfort level and stability the U.S. provides to investors.

From the master list of stocks, individual issues are bought and sold depending on these market overreactions. Armed with the knowledge of an entity's long-term viability, prospects, and plans, REA's portfolio managers do not hesitate to take advantage of growth opportunities. To achieve proper diversification, REA portfolios typically contain 20 to 25 stocks. Turnover is usually modest, but may vary from year to year. With a portfolio of growth stocks, volatility can be expected to be slightly greater than the S&P 500.

IV. SUMMARY—GET ON THE TRAIN

Despite the growth that has taken place over the past 24 years in this firm, little has changed with the founder. While he good-naturedly concedes that a couple of inches have been added to his waistline and a few amplifications to his eyeglasses, his investment philosophy remains precisely the same. Ask him the question, what is the best thing I can do with my money?, and the answer will be identical to what it was in 1969: buy common stocks.

REA's goal is simple and straightforward: to make money for its clients. According to Engemann and his investment management team, the best way to provide superior financial returns over the long term is to own stocks of well-managed, rapidly growing companies. The key is in those last five words. As Engemann pointed out, "If you own the stocks of crummy companies, you're going to have a crummy investment." At REA, the objective is to find the very best companies—companies whose earnings can be expected to grow in a consistent and sustainable manner over many years.

In his typically optimistic style, Engemann believes the outlook for equities is very positive, especially in an environment of low inflation and low bond yields. The aging baby boomers, who are moving into their prime savings age bracket, will provide the capital for investment in the future. Clearly the trend in interest rates has been downward since the early 1980s, but to get a better picture, Engemann suggests looking at the big picture (see Exhibit 5–2).

A glimpse at the 200-year span of bond yields indicates that today's 7 percent yields on long-term Treasury bonds are high in historical terms. Quick calculations show such yields have existed during only a small portion of the 200-year period. During the bulk

EXHIBIT 5–2
Two Hundred Years of Bond Yields (Percentage of Time That Bond Yields Were at a Given Level)

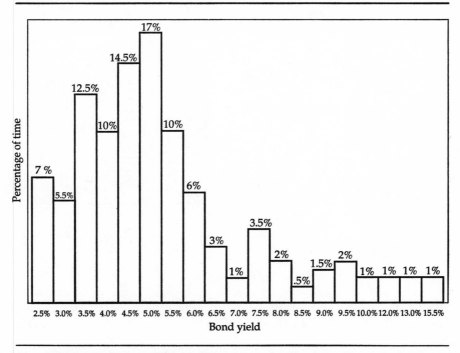

Source: Sidney Homer and Richard Sylla, *A History of Interest Rates.* 3rd ed. Copyright © 1991, Rutgers University Press, 1991.

of the time, 82.5 percent, yields were equal to or lower than 6 percent.

According to Engemann, our perception of what constitutes low interest rates is skewed by recent history. Rates of 10 percent are the anomaly, not 5 percent rates. The high returns seen in the past simply will not be sustainable in an environment of low inflation, making stocks, particularly growth stocks, a far more attractive alternative.

The current fear that P/Es are too high is also based on recent history rather than on long-term history or logic. In the chart, "Comparisons of Bond Yields With P/E Ratios," (Exhibit 5–3),

EXHIBIT 5–3
Comparison of Bond Yields with P/E Ratios

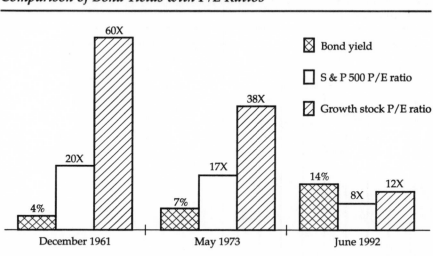

Source: Edward M. Kerschner, PaineWebber, Inc.

there are three snapshots of prior relationships between bond yields, the P/E ratio of the S&P 500, and the P/E ratio of growth stocks.

Two of the periods, December 1961 and May 1973, were times of low inflation. In contrast, in June 1982, interest rates and inflation were abnormally high. When bonds have high yields, like the 14 percent of 1982, the S&P P/E is relatively low, and growth stocks command little in the way of a premium to the S&P. However, in the early 1960s, bond yields were only 4 percent, while the S&P P/E ratio was 20X, and many growth stocks sold at 60X earnings. In between the two was May 1973, when bonds yielded 7 percent, with the S&P 500 selling at 17X. Meanwhile, growth stocks commanded multiples of 38X earnings.

The point? If bond yields return to a more normal level of 5 to 6 percent, the appropriate S&P 500 multiple would be in the high teens, and growth stocks could be double that at 35 to 40 times earnings.

Engemann cannot be dislodged off his positive pedestal. He

always returns to the same theme: "The best way to build wealth is through common stocks of rapidly growing companies, and unless you believe in the future, you'll never buy those stocks which will provide that wealth." Thus, his firm is best suited for you optimists at heart: those willing to own, through thick and thin, America's premier companies. It is difficult to imagine what possible economic, political, or social event would ruffle Engemann's growth-camp feathers.

According to Roger Engemann, Chicken Little has grown up. We see him every day—he works for the financial press. Every day the TV, business, and newspaper commentaries try to scare investors out of their wits. And unfortunately, sometimes they succeed—especially with today's nervous and hot money investors. REA believes an investor should not look at his portfolio every three minutes, three hours, or three days. At the most, a cursory review should be done every three months. In REA's eyes, even quarterly reviews might be viewed as excessive.

Engemann cautions investors not to put a performance time line or schedule on stocks. They move up when you least expect it under their own time schedule. He used this as a simple comparison: "Look at the stock market as a train sitting on the tracks. You can see where the tracks head, but what you don't know is the time of departure. The important point is to *get on* the train—and enjoy the ride."

Chapter Six

Fisher Investments

"You'll know one's true being by his deeds, not his words."

Unknown

Several thousand avowed value investment advisory firms do business in the United States today, but few carry their investment philosophies into their daily lives. Kenneth L. Fisher, founder of Fisher Investments, Inc., does. He is the ultimate bargain shopper, whether he is buying an underfollowed and undervalued small capitalization stock or consumer goods for his family. Although Fisher has the financial capability to purchase almost any consumer amenity, he prides himself on his bargain purchases. For example, during the interview for this book, he proudly boasted of the $200 lizard skin cowboy boots he purchased *used*, but virtually unworn, at Value Village for a staggering $8 and the car he had purchased for his family—an 11-year-old Volvo station wagon with under 100,000 miles.

Clearly, Ken Fisher does not fit the normal adviser mold. This man is an independent thinker with a unique investment philosophy and strategy. Where did he pick up this discount orientation toward life and the investment world? This trait can be traced back to his upbringing.

I. HISTORY

Fisher, the son of Philip A. Fisher, one of the legendary pioneers of the growth stock school of investing, evolved into value investing while he was young. It was a way to establish himself as his own person—apart from the far-reaching shadow of his friendly but formidable father. His father, even today known as San Francisco's most famous investment guru and highlighted in John Train's classic *The Money Masters* (which surveys the investment philosophies and strategies of nine of the all-time great stock market operators), encouraged his son to develop his own way of investing. Unlike many wealthy children, Fisher was expected to stand on his own feet and not ride the coattails of his father's success and notoriety. The casual observer would assume that he was taking the easy street following in his father's footsteps. Nothing could be further from the truth. The sugar-coated silver spoon was removed from this boy's mouth at an early age. From working on construction jobs to fund his business (where he lost part of a finger) to developing his clientele, Fisher was expected to earn his own way.

After graduating with a degree in economics from Humboldt State University, Fisher went to work for his father's investment firm. He branched off on his own in 1973, a mere 18 months after joining his father. He remembered, "From the beginning I just felt uncomfortable in the family business environment. I knew I had to be my own person."

While operating his small investment advisory firm during the next five years, Fisher refined the basic philosophy that today is Fisher Investments. During those years, he cast about with a lot of different activities and approaches. Not only did new business not come easily, but it was very difficult to shake the investment community's perception that Fisher, although independent, still needed his father's tutelage and direction. For example, when proposing an investment idea to a pension plan, the trustees or manager of the plan would say something like, "What does your father think of your recommendation?" While attempting to mask his growing impatience, he would explain that his father had nothing to do with the idea and would not be reviewing the merit or risks associated with the investment proposal. The investment community was slow to accept this independence.

Strange as it may sound, Fisher's evolution into small capitalization value began with lessons he learned while doing some small-scale packaging of venture capital deals. Fisher learned that venturists often priced deals based not on future forecasts of earnings (because they knew they couldn't really forecast five years of future profit margins for a start-up), but on estimates of future revenues (how big they hoped the companies would be). The venturists then compared those revenues to the revenues of existing firms to justify pricing.

Fisher wondered about extending this venture capital-based revenue analysis. Why not just seek overlooked areas where stocks had fallen out of favor—you could buy companies at the same market capitalizations the venturists were paying, but where the revenues were already there and you didn't have to forecast future growth. If corresponding profits were also present, you had a low P/E stock; if they weren't, you could analyze for the basic elements of a turnaround that would generate the future earnings, which would mean future profits and future low P/Es. Fisher was confident that it was a lot easier to analyze the elements necessary to a turnaround of a big company than to play the venturists' game of looking at a group of managers and technology and guessing how big a firm they could make.

Meanwhile, Fisher had stumbled on PPG Industries. It had fallen heavily into disfavor during the 1973–75 recession, and as Fisher put it, "was basically lost between the cracks on Wall Street." A huge company with $2 billion in sales, it was a leader or the dominant vendor in the flat glass, chlor-alkali chemicals, industrial coatings, and continuous strand fiberglass markets; Fisher knew this must be a valuable entity. Yet PPG's stock had fallen low enough to render this huge firm a small capitalization stock. PPG was so poorly treated by the Street that by 1975 the company basically gave up on any real investor relations efforts. It was virtually impossible to talk to management about what they were doing. Fisher liked this because he knew that if they did well, the Street would be caught totally unaware.

As Fisher researched the stock further, talking to customers, competitors, and suppliers, a picture emerged of a poorly regarded firm that was actually quite strong in everything it did, was getting stronger, and was exceptionally well-managed. Fisher's father, who was exceptionally good at analyzing companies, passed on this skill and ability to his son. Fisher fell in love and sold the idea of buying PPG stock to everyone he could find. PPG set Fisher about the philosophical quest that would become Fisher Investments, which in a simple sense is trying to take advantage of

the inherent spread in value that exists when the following dichotomy presents itself:

- Unpopular stocks of above-average quality companies.
- Small capitalization stocks of huge companies—firms that
  sell at very low ratios of market capitalization to sales size.

Fisher called this, "small caps, but big, good companies." The
efficient market shouldn't allow such stocks, and to the extent
they exist, they do so in violation of the concepts of modern
portfolio theory. As he sold investors on the ideas behind why
PPG should do well, Fisher fashioned the basic rationale of price/
sales ratios—that a stock selling at a low market capitalization
relative to its total revenues (with some adjustment for the type of
industry involved) is by definition an unpopular company. It is
similar to the popularized price/earnings ratio except that the
denominator is replaced with sales. As Fisher saw it, if the Street
wouldn't pay much for a dollar of revenue, it thought poorly of the
firm. If the firm then did well, the Street would be surprised, and
the stock would rise. Backed by over eight theoretical and academic studies, the price-to-sales tool is a superior valuation assessment instrument because it measures the expectation the market has for a specific stock.

While the same point could be made about P/Es, Fisher knew
that either through recession or company-specific events, good
firms are sometimes profitless—and in these cases P/Es don't
work. As Fisher put it, "At times some of the most interesting
huge companies have no P/E at all because for whatever reason,
temporarily there isn't any E (earnings), but there is always a
price/sales ratio."

PPG was a staggering success for Fisher, almost instantly rising
dramatically in price and paying a fat dividend. The $150 million
market capitalization turned into a $500 million capitalization, and
then a $1 billion capitalization, and finally a $3 billion capitalization when he sold it. Today it is a $6 billion capitalization and
for a decade has been an institutionally accepted mainstream
stock. The PPG experience not only set Fisher Investments' early
direction, but its continued success provided ongoing inspiration.

In the next few years, Fisher succeeded with a number of low
price/sales ratio stocks, most notably Nucor Corporation in 1976.

While today Nucor is widely noted as America's top steel manufacturer, then it was largely unknown, having not yet sufficiently
distanced itself from its prior bankruptcy and conglomerate days.
Fisher was instantly impressed, both with CEO Ken Iverson and
Nucor's commercialization of new, low-cost steel technology.
Within a few years the stock was up 10-fold, and Nucor was clearly
sparking a revolution in the way steel was made. These successes
reinforced Fisher's methodology.

He began applying price/sales ratios (which he abbreviated to
PSRs) to all types of stocks. By 1978, he was routinely applying the
PSR concept to technology stocks and benefited from the bull
market in that sector which started then and ran until 1983. It
seemed odd buying technology stocks at value prices, but it
brought returns with lower risks. Also in 1978, Fisher began to get
his first fully discretionary accounts where he could buy and sell
without the clients' prior approval—the beginnings of Fisher Investments as it is today.

By 1983, the performance that came with value-based technology companies led Fisher to start writing his first book, *Super
Stocks*, which was published by Dow Jones-Irwin in 1984. In it,
Fisher not only introduced the world to price/sales ratios in detail,
extolling the virtues of stocks selling at low ratios of market capitalization to total revenue, but he also sternly warned the world of
the upcoming dangers of high-flying technology stocks that sold at
high price/sales ratios. The next two years would prove those
warnings prophetic. The first half of *Super Stocks* was devoted to
price/sales ratios, the second half to the methodology of research-
ing a company. The book was the most successful stock market
book of the year, selling more than 30,000 copies, and was included on many lists of most important investment books, including *Barron's* and Standard & Poor's. Its reputation propelled the
firm.

Another important milestone came in 1983 when Fisher met and
hired Jeff Silk, who was introduced to Fisher by a former mutual
professor. Silk's energy and enthusiasm were even greater than
Fisher's and pushed Fisher further. Fisher saw in Silk a rare quality
that he described as, "Being one of the few smart people in the
world who can take a two-by-four between the eyes and never
stop moving forward." Silk spearheaded much of the historical

research that went into *Super Stocks,* and after assignments in each of the varying parts of Fisher Investments' business, he eventually became a shareholder in the firm, a senior vice president, and director of operations.

Shortly after meeting Silk, Fisher met another key player in the firm's evolution—through a fluke. In the early 1980s, Robert Toms worked for Fisher for a short time, during which he proudly extolled the virtues of his son, Joe, "the stockbroker." Joseph Toms, young and green at 25, had been working for a southern California-based institutional research boutique and had hoped to "sell" Fisher. Joseph Toms called on Fisher at the senior Toms' introduction and followed up with a thank-you letter. Fisher deplores the use of the word *I,* and Toms' letter was full of *I*s. In typical, curt, Fisher fashion, he circled all the *I*s in the letter, attached it to a copy of a Dale Carnegie page explaining why *I* is a dirty word, and sent it back.

Fisher figured and hoped he would never hear from Toms again. A week later the young man was on the phone, asking for a job and explaining that he was green and really would benefit from an employer who would be brutally honest in showing Toms what he needed to do to hone himself.

Fisher has been brutally honest ever since, and Toms keeps getting better. Originally, Fisher saw a lot of himself in Toms: bright, hard working, driven, intuitive, and a fast learner who always benefited from his own mistakes and landed on his feet. But Fisher also saw Toms as having more natural polish and self-confidence than he had.

The three, Fisher, Silk, and Toms, became a trio, with Silk being Mr. Inside; Toms often dealing with the outside world; and Fisher leading as pioneer and ultimate decision maker. Like Silk, after holding stints in most parts of the firm, today Toms is also a shareholder and senior vice president, as well as running the firm's activities in market research and client services.

As these three came together, two other things happened. First, with time under its belt and a relatively unique investment style that focused on unpopular stocks of fairly large companies, the firm naturally started to focus on the institutional world that liked to hire specialty managers and had relatively little exposure to smaller-value stocks. That shift in focus away from individuals and toward institutions has continued. Today the firm is almost solely institutional, being the largest vendor of a pure small capitalization value style in the corporate pension plan market.

And *Forbes* happened. Fisher met James W. Michaels, who for two decades had been the editor of *Forbes*, and built a relationship with him through the early drafts of Fisher's book, which Michaels liked a great deal. Michaels suggested changes and research; ultimately, in the volume's introduction, Fisher formally credited Michaels' inspiration for two chapters.

Coming out of this relationship, Fisher started suggesting column ideas to Michaels and in July 1984 wrote his first *Forbes* column. Since then, his column has appeared in every other issue of *Forbes*. Originally, Fisher was recommending growth stocks selling at low valuations. Soon he broadened the focus, and it became and has remained the "Portfolio Strategy" column, covering topics all over the investment spectrum, including major calls in market direction. Fisher is extremely proud of his caution before the 1987 break, his outright bold bearishness before the 1989 broad market peak, and his extreme bullishness in late 1990 and into 1991 as that new bull market began.

Fisher wrote a second market book in 1987—*The Wall Street Waltz*—which sprang from his familiarity (via *Forbes*) with covering a lot in a one-page format. In this book he took his favorite 90 charts from all of financial history and coupled each with a simple one-page story that told where the chart came from, what it meant, and why it was important for thinking about the future of the financial markets.

By 1992, Fisher Investments had become a mature institutional research boutique. With 29 people managing almost three quarters of a billion dollars—and all solely engaged in small capitalization value equities—Fisher Investments had evolved from a bootstrap operation to a national leader. From its start as the casting about of the son of a growth stock guru—who felt compelled to go his own way to establish his own identity—the firm has evolved into a pioneer whose views and philosophies are often synonymous with defining the institutional world's perceptions of small capitalization value investing. It has evolved from a one-man show to a firm where Fisher is CEO and is proud that his people are "better than I am—and that we have more bodies, more degrees, more graduate degrees, computers, and computer systems than any-one, anywhere in small cap value."

II. PHILOSOPHY

Over time, and as a function of its increased capabilities over time, Fisher investments has refined its definition of small capitalization value.

Academic research into stock market returns has demonstrated that the two most important determinants of a stock's perfor-mance are market capitalization and valuation. The market's re-turn over the past 20 years can be explained by these two variables. Fisher Investments looks at these two variables in a unique way and sees the market as being made up of four distinct quadrants, based on these two variables. Specifically, if arrayed from biggest to smallest (the vertical axis on Exhibit 6–1), stocks can be sepa-rated into the *big capitalization* world and the *small capitalization* world. From there, both groups can be split by a valuation mea-sure (price to book). The mid to high half of valuation is referred to as the *growth* end, and the mid to low half is referred to as the *value* end. The result is four distinct quadrants: big capitalization value, big capitalization growth, small capitalization value, and small capitalization growth. Fisher Investments is a small capitalization value manager.

The essence of Fisher's small capitalization value philosophy is that in order to achieve superior, long-term returns, it is necessary to identify and purchase small capitalization companies whose futures are likely to exceed expectations. More specifically, that superior long-term results are derived from taking advantage of the pricing mechanism of the market—of the relationship between investor expectations and eventual reality. Investors purchase a stock with an expectation of a future reality. If the ensuing reality is better than expectations, the stock will rise. If reality falls short of expectations, the stock will go down.

This interplay of expectations versus reality is more compelling in the small capitalization value world because there are more inefficiencies to exploit. Of the four quadrants, the small capitali-zation value quadrant has the least Wall Street analyst coverage.

EXHIBIT 6–1
Top 2,000 Market Capitalization Stocks

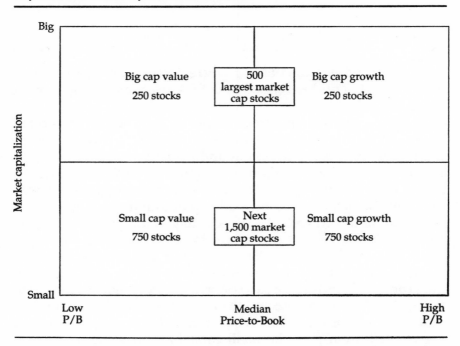

Few analysts follow these stocks; therefore, an investment firm must initiate its own research. The small capitalization value quadrant can be seen as a sort of "penalty box" in the sense that it's not where you want to be if you are the CEO of a company. Within small capitalization, value companies have low expectations and growth companies have high expectations attached to them. Therefore, within small capitalization, the value universe provides more room for reality to exceed expectations, sending stock prices up. One of Fisher's basic beliefs is that the lower the expectation one has for a stock's success, the higher the probability a positive surprise will result. This is borne out by historical evidence which shows that small capitalization value stocks outperform all other asset classes, including common stocks as a whole, over the long term.

As noted, Fisher measures expectations in terms of the price/

sales ratio (PSR). To identify companies whose future is brighter than expected, the firm looks for quality in a company's strategic position relative to its specific industry as well as its financial strength—both of which will produce strong future growth. Quality companies of which little is expected will achieve better than expected margins and/or growth, thus producing superior gains, allowing the company to work its way out of the penalty box—because ultimately Fisher wants its companies to evolve in size and valuations into being big capitalization growth stocks (see Exhibit 6–2).

III. STRATEGY/PROCESS

Fisher's strategy is bottom-up, based on individual stock selection as illustrated in Exhibit 6–3. The firm first narrows the stock universe quantitatively to isolate low-expectation, small capitalization stocks with strong balance sheets. It then does in-depth qualitative research to identify companies in the remaining group whose prospects are better than expected, for whom reality will exceed the market's current expectations. It gleans the best from both methodologies—the time-saving feature of the quantitative process and the beyond-the-numbers aspect of qualitative research.

A. *Quantitative*

Step one: capitalize on the "small cap effect." Fisher starts by screening the Standard & Poor's Compustat database by market capitalization. He discards the 500 largest and concentrates on the next 1,500 stocks by market capitalization. This allows the firm to benefit from the small capitalization effect without sacrificing liquidity.

Step two: identify low-expectation stocks. Within this small capitalization universe, a further screen is done for the low three deciles (lowest 30 percent) of PSRs, which represent less than 2 percent of the value of the total market. The key characteristics of the portfolio center on the effect the PSR produces. Since the

EXHIBIT 6–2
Market Capitalization Chart

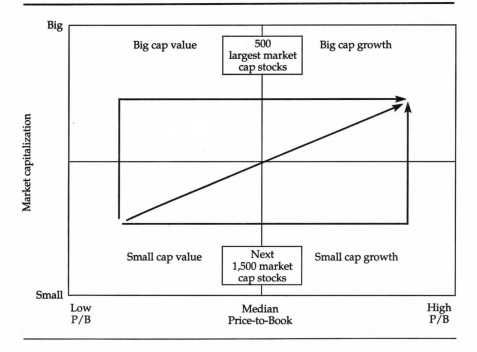

ratio centers on sales and not current earnings, the companies purchased for the portfolio have wide earnings variability. The PSR captures companies with a range of profitability pictures— from no current earnings to explosive earnings growth—and is thus better suited to analyzing small capitalization stocks. In addition, it differentiates portfolios from other managers (including other small capitalization managers) who focus solely on the P/E. Above all, the PSR serves as a quantitative measure of expectation. The less investors are willing to pay for $1 of revenue, the lower the expectation they have for the stock.

Not surprisingly, when investors as a group are overly confident of the market's prospects, the number of candidates is not only lean but the quality of identified stocks is poor. Put simply, the higher-quality small companies move into the larger capitalization and/or small capitalization growth quadrants, leaving the

EXHIBIT 6–3
Overview of Investment Decision Process

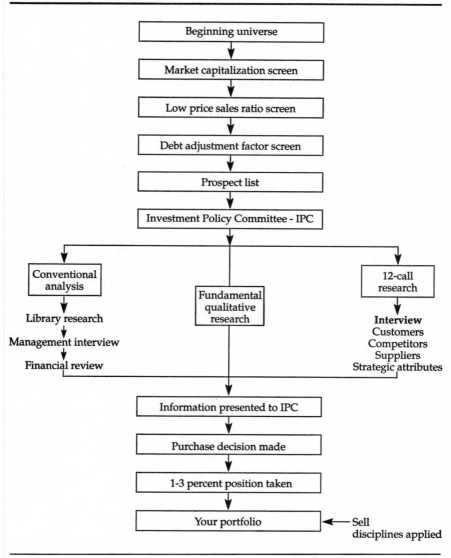

junk—the less desirable companies—behind. Conversely, when the investment community reeks with pessimism, Fisher's small capitalization value quadrant is teeming with high-quality companies.

Step three: find financial strength. Everyone always has known that the earnings of a heavily leveraged company should be worth less than the earnings of a comparable but less leveraged company—but no one asked: "how much less?" until Fisher came along. At Fisher Investments, all low PSR stocks are subjected to a unique and proprietary balance sheet screen called the debt adjustment factor (DAF). The DAF assesses both short-term and long-term debt plus cash flow and depreciation in a single liquidity measure to identify companies with not only extremely strong balance sheets, but with balance sheet strength relative to their valuations. The DAF is superior to the widely used debt-to-equity ratio because it does not eliminate companies that may have a large debt load but will survive because of their high excess free cash flow, a large working capital base, and a decent depreciation schedule. For example, if a company's earnings are 10 percent and debt is costing only 8 percent, then it is worthwhile to carry the debt leverage. The DAF points out when a seemingly cheap stock isn't cheap at all because of its excessive debt load. This step eliminates potential solvency risks and leaves a list of companies that have the finances to compete effectively in their fields—a necessary element to be considered a quality company.

Once Fisher has narrowed the number of haystacks, the firm begins the qualitative process that ultimately finds the needles. Knowing that over 50 percent of the stocks located in the small capitalization value quadrant will remain as garbage stocks, Fisher and his team attempt to determine if, in fact, there is a reason for a company to be destined to the small capitalization value quadrant. In other words, while the small capitalization value quadrant offers the most potential, it is also the graveyard for disasters.

B. Qualitative

Step one: conventional analysis. Each stock is assigned to an analyst who gathers corporate documents, reviews a library search for everything in print on the firm for three years, and talks with management about the firm's history, goals, competitive position, and strategies for the future. The analyst then assigns points for issues of concern across a formal spectrum of conventional analytical arenas. For example, problems hidden in a firm's financial footnotes would receive negative points. A well-conceived strategy for future improvement might receive positive points. The point totals for each stock are a conventional overall qualitative assessment of the firm and its industry position.

Step two: 12-call research. The 12-call research process involves interviewing customers, competitors, and suppliers to ascertain a firm's strategic competitive position. The process looks for signs—direct from Main Street—pointing to one or more strategic attributes normally associated with firms with a natural competitive advantage in their fields, including low-cost production or distribution, unique distribution system, unique functional niche, brand name dominance, superior service reputation, high relative market share, regional dominance—attributes which are unique to the firm. Basically, the 12-call research process attempts to identify those companies that have the potential to move out of the lower, small value quadrant.

Among Fisher Investments' staff are eight 12-call consultants, strategically situated across the country. Typically former journalists living in rural communities, these people perform this proprietary, 12-call process. (Fisher has found urban 12-callers tend to let the negative daily life struggles of living in the city influence their analysis of even the quality companies.)

Twelve-callers are assigned prospective companies that have made it through the quantitative screens. The 12-caller typically identifies four customers, four competitors, and four suppliers, who are then interviewed by telephone. The customers are asked *buy* questions like: "What sometimes makes you buy from company A and other times from company B? How might that change in the future? How are your buy decisions different from others in the industry?" Competitors are asked *sell* questions: "Why do you sometimes win when competing against company A and other times lose? What are you doing to change that?" Suppliers are the most difficult to talk to but often provide the best information. They are difficult because they are often afraid they could lose a sale if their comments get back to their customers. They are informative because they are analysts—they thrive or die based on how well they understand their customers' needs. They are asked all the questions normally associated with a security analyst (except for earnings per share questions) like: "Who is doing well and who is doing poorly and why? How might that change in the future? Who is the biggest? Have they been gaining or losing share? Who has cost advantages? Can anyone consistently buy your cheapest grade materials?"

Sometimes a 12-call must be customized to a firm or industry and takes more or fewer than 12 completed calls. For instance, a firm with no competitors might have an ideal strategic position warranting investment, despite the fact that there are no competitor calls. In some fields, such as retailing, more than four customers must be interviewed because single customer comments tend to be spurious. Some suppliers have no useful information about a company's competitors, and often this can't be ascertained until after calls are completed, requiring even more calls to complete the process.

The consultants assemble their findings into a 12-call report. The report then is given to an analyst who summarizes what the customers, competitors, and suppliers have said about the strategic position of the firm. Do their comments point to a low-cost producer? A firm with high market share or improving margins on sales or, perhaps, to merely a "me-too" firm? The summary is then approved by another analyst and is taken to the weekly investment policy committee (IPC) meeting to be merged with conventional analysis.

Fisher believes the 12-call system to be superior to Wall Street research because of the focus on the people closest to the particular company—customers and suppliers. By comparing the 12-call information to what the company's executives are saying, Fisher can determine if the management perceives the necessary attributes for change. Fisher calculates the 12-call process adds approximately 1 percent annually to the overall rate of return for Fisher portfolios. The six-member IPC hears results of the 12-call report and conventional analysis. It routinely decides to purchase the stock of companies that score well on conventional points and have demonstrable strategic competitive advantages as determined through the 12-call process.

The end result is a portfolio of small capitalization stocks with strong balance sheets, selling at valuation discounts. These companies, which average close to $1 billion in sales, need to bring these sales to the bottom line. The companies have capable managements who use their firms' strategic advantages toward strengthening position and growing the company. Currently, Fisher holds 75 such companies in its client portfolio, which means 1 of 10 of its 750 stock universe makes its cut.

IV.   SELL SYSTEMS

As important as a good buy process is the ability to maximize gains and minimize losses through a wise sell process. In reality, it's harder to know when to sell than what to buy. That is why Fisher has developed a disciplined, objective process that protects total return.

System one: winners.   Target pricing allows winners to run while protecting gains. It ensures Fisher Investments doesn't fall in love with any one company just as it reaches its price peak. When a stock is purchased, a target price is calculated. The target price pinpoints where a stock would be more popular than the market, and hence more risky. The target price takes into account the specific stock's debt-adjusted PSR and weights it against a formula based on combining a composite of the Value Line composite index and the company's specific industry's debt-adjusted PSR, P/E, and P/B. The target price is continually updated based on fluctuations of the stock, the company's finances, and the market's overall level and condition. If a stock is sold and no worthy replacement is identified, Fisher holds the proceeds in cash. This is how asset allocation is adjusted over time.

System two: losers.   The "losers" selling system allows for normal fluctuation in a stock's price but forces a quick sale if a stock performs poorly. This discipline ensures that Fisher cuts its losses short. This is a two-step process to identify mistakes early. The first step is triggered when a stock falls 15 percent relative to the market. The company is then reassigned to a new analyst who

EXHIBIT 6–4
Big Capitalization Value versus Growth (Three-Year Value Return minus Growth Return—Three-Year Rolling Periods)

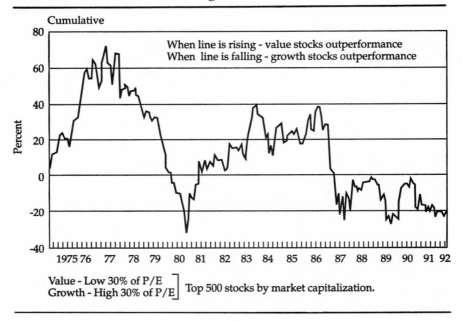

Value - Low 30% of P/E
Growth - High 30% of P/E   Top 500 stocks by market capitalization.

rechecks with fresh eyes the original research done on the company. By bringing in a new analyst, natural human bias/blindness is caught early. If flaws are discovered in the original research, the stock is sold. If the company's advantages are reaffirmed, the stock is held, but if the stock falls another 15 percent in absolute terms, it triggers an automatic sell.

System three: laggards. Opportunity cost is a serious consideration. This system maintains focus on the rate of return of each position. By pruning poorly performing stocks, cash is redeployed more productively. Stagnation can hurt as much as losses, due to missed opportunities while assets are tied up in poor performers. Stocks are given two years from purchase date in the overall Fisher Investments portfolio to outperform the Value Line composite. If they don't, they are sold.

EXHIBIT 6–5
*Small Capitalization Value versus Growth (Three-Year Value Return
minus Growth Return—Three-Year Rolling Periods)*

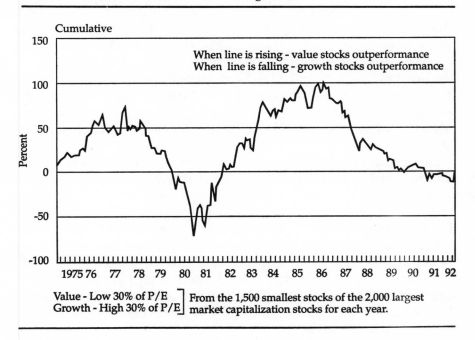

Value - Low 30% of P/E ⎤ From the 1,500 smallest stocks of the 2,000 largest
Growth - High 30% of P/E ⎦ market capitalization stocks for each year.

System four: changing fundamentals. This mechanism
ensures Fisher owns only what fits the firm's definition of quality.
It allows flexibility in a constantly changing world, so positions
can be sold before they become losers. Any company can change
dramatically through restructuring, acquisition, and so forth, and
these changes can have a dramatic impact on the company's performance and competitive edge. If there are any severe, negative
changes, the stock is sold.

V. SUMMARY

In the early 1980s, the small capitalization value style performed
above both large capitalization value and growth stocks (see Exhibits 6–4 and 6–5). But from 1986–91, this quadrant did not keep

pace with the overall market run-up. Investors were extremely disappointed with the investment community's lack of interest in small value stocks.

But since October 1991, the tide has quickly reversed itself. For the first six months of 1992, both the small and large capitalization value stocks have made up a lot of lost ground. While the average growth stocks, which include America's favorite companies, have declined between 10 and 20 percent, the value sector has risen 8 to 15 percent. This represents an almost 20 percent spread or differential between value and growth stocks. Although it is too early to identify a trend, recent market action signifies a major shift to value.

Some managers have no particular style, and others are very stylized. Fisher Investments is a highly disciplined, stylized manager specializing in small capitalization value stocks—which over the longest periods measurable have been the market's best performers. Most investors, institutional and retail alike, have very little exposure to small capitalization value. Being one of the pioneers in this area, having specialized in it far longer than most firms and with the largest dedicated research effort aimed at small capitalization value, Fisher Investments offers the advantage of high potential returns along with the natural volatility that comes with any specialized style.

Chapter Seven

Fox Asset Management

"If you pay too much for a great company, you will probably lose money. If you buy a mediocre company cheap enough, you will probably make money."

Gerald Loeb

These two sentences, taken from Gerald Loeb's 1955 classic investment book, *Battle for Investment Survival*, are forever engraved in J. Peter Skirkanich's mind. It was the first investment book he read and, even today, it defines his firm's approach to managing assets.

Since 1985, Fox Asset Management, under Skirkanich's direction, has employed a value approach. Fox eschews the "tulip bulb mania"[1] investment strategy in which today's top gun equity managers sport some very fancy returns from the current manias such as the biotechs in 1991. In the end, they will crash and burn just like their brethren of the past. Skirkanich explained his investment approach with these words: "We are lonely, long-distance runners; this is a mind-set which is more conducive to long-term investment success; and a key factor in our investment approach. The high-risk takers garnering most of the media's attention are a world apart from our approach."

I. HISTORY

Peter Skirkanich first became interested in the stock market during a Christmas break from college. He read an article about RCA and its new product—the color TV. Teetering between paying for

---

[1] In Holland in the 1520s the speculation and optimism in tulip growth became so excessive that one tulip bulb equaled the selling price of one acre of land.

another semester at school or putting his savings into RCA stock, Peter opted for staying in school. Over the next four years, he saw the RCA stock, much to his chagrin, quadruple in value. The stock market seed was planted, but it was not harvested for another 10 years.

Graduating from Wharton School and wanting to get into the investment business, he worked briefly for a public accounting firm. He joined the State Department in 1967, where he spent two and a half years in Latin America. It was in Chile that he learned an important investment lesson, the impact of inflation on one's investment. Watching the impact of inflation of 35 to 40 percent per year provided an excellent real experience to go along with his academic training and public accounting exposure.

After his stint with the State Department, Skirkanich returned to the United States and finally entered the investment world as a financial analyst with Bache & Company. Desiring to manage investments directly, he later joined Kidder, Peabody and Shearson American Express before becoming a managing director with Dreman Value Management.

To maintain the medium-sized firm environment and to get away from the hubbub of New York, he started Fox Asset Management in Little Silver, New Jersey. The firm has grown to include six other investment professionals (John Liang, Paul Stach, Russell Tompkins, Gavin Gilmor, Jerry Fisher, and Terry Potter), a trader with 25 years of experience, and some talented younger people. Together they manage assets in excess of $900 million for clients throughout the United States.

II.   PHILOSOPHY

Fox's disciplined and distinctive investment philosophy is grounded in academic research, beginning with the work of Benjamin Graham, David L. Dodd, and Paul F. Miller, Jr. Simply put, value investing requires a disciplined evaluation of companies; acquisition of stock occurs *only* when the price appears to be at a material discount to the intrinsic or fair market value.

Miller, in 1966, completed an extensive and conclusive study of the S&P 500's return record from 1948 to 1964. He divided all companies listed in the S&P's composite with over $150 million in sales into five groups on the basis of their past price/earnings (P/E ratio) rank. Each year these quintiles were reestablished on the basis of their changing earnings record.

The results were clear, as shown in Exhibit 7–1. Performance returns varied inversely with the level of their respective P/E multiple. The darlings of the investing public—the highest P/E stocks—demonstrated an average annual appreciation of 7.7 percent, while the bottom or unloved quintile of the S&P stocks returned an astounding 18.4 percent annual rate, nearly two and a half times as much. Miller also found these "dogs" (those with the lowest P/Es) outperformed in 12 out of the 17 years, while the stocks with the highest P/Es—the top quintile—performed best in only one year. Subsequent studies by David Dreman and others support the success of the low P/E approach to equity investing.

Fox performed prior studies of investment results relating to cash flow valuation which combined with the above studies to form the basis for the firm's equity approach. According to Skirkanich, investing is a way of life and a life-long pursuit. It involves following one basic path, the discipline that you can live with through thick or thin. While that discipline allows for a great deal of individuality, the philosophy and discipline you choose must be clearly defined and constant.

In discussing investment philosophy, Skirkanich commented, "To achieve long-term performance, first you must have total and unbending confidence in your investment strategy. The acid test is which strategy allows you enough comfort during the inevitable, painful, down markets to stay with the long-term game plan." He continued, "An investment strategy is not worth much if you constantly change due to a lack of underlying confidence or comfort. This is the difference between investing and playing the market."

Second, like many of the great investors with superior track records, Fox's attention to risk makes it stand out. Fox does not rely on pure intelligence or large capital outlays for outside research. In making his point, Skirkanich commented,

Huntington Hartford, heir to the huge A&P fortune, had access to the smartest investment minds in the world. Yet, without apparent regard for risk, he oversaw one of the most outstanding records of dissipating wealth of anyone in history. Unlike Mr. Hartford, the best investors

EXHIBIT 7–1
Average Price Increases per Year (1948–64)

P/E Quintile	Price Increase (percent)
1st (high P/E)	7.7
2nd	9.2
3rd	12.0
4th	12.8
5th (low P/E)	18.4

Source: Drexel & Co., Philadelphia, Monthly Review, 1966.

have a great respect for the preservation and building of capital. An investment strategy should be designed to control risk as the first step.

In defining risk, Fox believes one of the most misunderstood factors is the lack of liquidity in many investments. Liquidity allows investors the opportunity to move out of an investment at their choosing. This ability is important in trying to control a loss, taking a gain where a valuation no longer makes sense, or in shifting a portfolio orientation as opportunities change. Many real estate investors have had to painfully relearn this lesson in recent years.

Skirkanich and his group at Fox have found that their value approach, where stock prices must be related to the underlying cash and earnings production of a company, provides a level of comfort. At Fox Asset Management, the investment committee is constantly comparing the potential rate of return to the relative return of lower-risk U.S. Treasuries (5- to 10-year maturities), as well as equity alternatives. Relating back to Loeb's quotation, buying a great company is not enough to ensure investment success—price (valuation) is an integral factor.

III. STRATEGY

A. Equity

Fox initially focuses on the amount and use of cash flow per share in a similar manner to Systematic's Ken Hackel. Specifically, the firm concentrates on earnings plus noncash expenses. Cash flow from operations defines a company's ability to maintain and increase its current capacity and efficiency, to invest in its future (acquisition or research and development), to pay interest and principal on debt, and perhaps most importantly, to increase dividends to investors.

In addition to the cash flow criteria, Fox also requires that its stock candidates sell at below-market P/E multiples. This adviser is very specific on how it defines value. All investment candidates must meet at least one of the following criteria:

1. Sell at a 20 percent discount to the S&P 500 on either a cash flow or earnings basis;
2. Offer a cash return of at least double the 5- to 10-year Treasury bond rates; or
3. Sell at a minimum 40 percent discount to its net asset value.

Unless Fox can build a portfolio of companies which offers a cash return of double the Treasury rate hurdle, its portfolio managers would rather maintain some portion of their client's capital in cash reserves. For example, if the 10-year Treasury bonds are yielding 7 percent, then the Fox hurdle rate for investments is 14 percent cash return. So, if its portfolio averages 5 times cash flow, the cash flow return is 20 percent $(100/5 = 20)$. Therefore, being fully invested is warranted, which is Fox's preferred asset allocation.

Historically, Fox has found that portfolios had a tendency to perform poorly when these valuation benchmarks are not met due to the inherent higher risk level. Specifically, either interest rates are too high and/or equity valuations are excessive. In other words, when Fox believes that achieving a premium return is not probable, its portfolio managers prefer to protect its clients' capital for another day when the risk/return characteristics are more favorable. For instance, in 1981, with Treasury bill rates soaring to 15 percent, the prime rate to 21 percent, and tax-free bond rates at 15 percent, achieving double those rates (their risk premium or hurdle rate) in the equity markets was impossible. Faced with similar future conditions, Fox's short-term cash holdings could run over 50 percent.

The companies included in the Fox portfolios have a history of increasing cash flow at a solid growth rate. Their current cash flow is also high relative to the current stock price (a low cash flow to price ratio). This discipline, historically as well as currently, generates a portfolio of companies with materially lower P/E ratios and significantly higher yields from dividends than the market averages—in Fox's view, a lower-risk portfolio with above-average return potential.

Fox monitors a universe of about 2,000 companies to find 75 to 100 qualifying candidates for use in the construction of client portfolios. Then it screens once more to identify the best cash flow growth prospects meeting the majority of these stock selection criteria:

- High cash flow per share.
- Consistent cash flow growth.
- Dividend yield materially above the market average.
- Consistent dividend growth.
- Sustainable dividend payout rate.
- Low price relative to earnings (low P/E ratio).
- High per-share working capital.
- Low debt to equity ratio.
- Favorable price relative to asset value.

From the pool of stocks meeting these criteria, 25 to 35 companies are selected for the client portfolios representing 15 to 20 industries. Each position typically makes up 2 to 4 percent of a portfolio. Fox does not get overly concerned about overweighting the client portfolios in one sector or industry (up to 10–12 percent). If the value is present and the fundamentals make sense, Fox will increase exposure to that particular industry.

Fox looks beyond U.S. borders for investment candidates. Typically, 20 percent of the holdings in Fox's client portfolios are foreign-based. Moreover, turnover in the Fox portfolios is one of the lowest among managers, running at 20 to 25 percent per year.

Fox is especially wary of companies growing at 20 to 25 percent annually and those loaded with debt. The real world, with its competitive pressures, does not allow that type of long-term growth. Therefore, buying a slower grower (8–10 percent) with an unleveraged balance sheet, consistent and growing cash flow, and a higher-than-average dividend rate is, in Fox's eyes, a less risky way of investing. On average, Fox's client portfolios have a debt level of less than 25 percent, substantially less than the debt level of the average stock in the S&P 500. These types of stocks tend to have less downside volatility.

Why are higher-than-average dividend yields and consistent dividend growth so important? From 1926 to 1991, fully one half of the total return from stocks has come from growing, reinvested dividends. Skirkanich gave this lucid example:

> Historically, the market has grown dividends at about a 5 percent annual rate. In other words, your income triples in 22 years. If you own companies which are growing dividends at 7 to 8 percent, your portfolio income triples in 16 years—six years less than on average stock in the S&P 500 index. Moving the figure to a 10 percent dividend growth rate (Fox's goal), your dividend income will triple in just 12 years. So, if you select high-quality stocks with dividend yields of 4 percent, in 12 years you'll have a 12 percent portfolio yield.

When asked why more investment managers do not use cash flow analysis, Skirkanich responded,

> Cash flow analysis has always been a part of the arsenal of most value investors, it only became the rage on Wall Street in the mid-1980s when LBO artists and investment bankers were calculating how much debt a company could carry in an attempt to win the bidding contest of their latest takeover attempt. The tool became even more perverted in the late 1980s when some of the bidding wars seemed to be dictated by takeover fees, not sensible investment merits. We use cash flow analysis to first, gauge our risk and second, to evaluate investment potential—the inverse of the speculator's approach.

In security analysis, cash flow analysis has always played second fiddle to growth equity analysis. The major tenet of the growth analysis school is being able to project future growth. Then given the assumed growth and an assumed interest rate environment, a stock's price can be determined. Over the long term, Fox finds this analysis to be very difficult, if not impossible. Fox's portfolio managers are skeptical of anyone's professed ability to consistently project both accurate growth rates and interest rates. Historically, over 30 percent of the Wall Street estimates are off by

30 percent or more. Skirkanich commented, "Based on these numbers, we think that pure growth analysis is a risky venture and prefer our valuation criteria as the primary stock selection tool for our client portfolios."

In addition to controlling risk through the purchase of mostly large capitalization, undervalued securities with consistent cash flow and dividend growth, Fox has two *critical* sell disciplines— one for the entire portfolio and the other for individual holdings:

1. For the entire portfolio, if the portfolio cash flow per share drops to less than twice the current treasury yield benchmark, positions must be sold until the remaining client portfolio is undervalued relative to current interest rates. This prevents Fox from being fully invested in an overvalued market.

2. If a specific portfolio equity holding is valued on a cash flow and price/earnings ratio basis above the broad market's (S&P 500) for a six-month period, it is sold.

B.   Fixed Income

Being characterized as a balanced manager (holding both stocks and bonds), Fox predominantly uses short- and intermediate-term bonds for its clients' fixed-income assets. Fox's fixed-income strategy is as defined as its equity strategy. Portfolio managers are not interested in risking capital in the long bond market. Why? Since World War II, long bonds have been just as volatile as stocks, but have offered substantially lower rates of returns. By monitoring maturities in the 2- to 10-year range, the bond portion of the portfolios provides stability (less volatility) to complement the equity side. As Russell Tompkins explained, "It is very important that our fixed-income strategy complements the equity strategy. Bonds should help control volatility in down markets, not add to it."

Skirkanich and his associates at Fox spend relatively little time attempting to project interest rates, the economy, or any financial market. Rather, they attempt to define the framework or volatility over the next 6 to 12 months and adjust their portfolios accordingly. Again, as with the selection of equities, the fixed-income strategies are grounded in preserving capital and reducing interest rate volatility. Fox assumes ongoing interest rate volatility. By keeping its fixed-income maturities short and actively managing

EXHIBIT 7–2
Sample Fixed-Income Portfolio (December 31, 1991)

	Percent of Portfolio Held in		
Treasury	Corporate	Cash	Foreign Government*
50%	31%	0%	19%

Yield to maturity	7.50%
Average coupon	8.82%
Average maturity	5 years 9 months
Average Moody's corporate rating	Aaa3
Duration	4.3 years

* Client directives permitting, 20% of total portfolio may be invested in short- to intermediate-term foreign government bonds.

the portfolios, Fox is able to take advantage of interest rate fluctuations. From 1960 to 1990, long-term U.S. Treasuries have subjected investors to 72 percent higher volatility than intermediate-term government bonds. Intermediate bonds had only one down year for the 30-year period 1960–90, while long-term bonds had nine losing years (25 percent of the time) over the same period. Those nine losing years had a combined loss of over 25 percent.

The fixed-income allocation is primarily made up of top-rated U.S. and foreign government bonds, investment grade corporate bonds, and occasionally a small portion of special situations. Skirkanich's experience in the foreign service has provided him special insight into the overseas bond markets. Also, each of Fox's senior people has had overseas experience. In Exhibit 7–2, Fox's sample fixed-income portfolio is illustrated. Currently, with over $600 million under management, 70 percent are balanced accounts, 20 percent equity-only accounts, and 10 percent fixed-income-only accounts.

IV. SUMMARY

Skirkanich and his team reiterate the idea of being comfortable with your investment philosophy and style no matter what the market presents to you. Second, as with many top-ranked investment firms, the concept of risk control is paramount in their investment decision-making process. Skirkanich commented, "We prepare for the worst, protecting our downside first. That is the main foundation of how we operate."

Skirkanich finds the current environment, with people moving assets into stocks on a "willy-nilly" basis and popularization of the saying "cash is trash," to be a bit disconcerting. The current thinking in the stock marketplace reminds him of the real estate market heyday (people blindly invested all their funds in real estate, eschewing stocks, as a matter of faith, not economics). How will this speculation ultimately be remedied? Skirkanich believes a good stock market correction will separate the real investors from the speculators . . . as it always has in the past.

In line with this thinking, Fox is not interested in attracting the fast money crowd to its firm. Skirkanich knows that its slow, methodical, low-turnover style will bore these people, who will probably seek more excitement elsewhere—at least until the next correction. The client portfolios are peppered with bland, lower-profile companies with strong balance sheets and dividend growth records. Because these companies are not part of the current hot investment themes, Fox is able to purchase these companies at very modest prices. Fox only wants clients that have a reasonable rate of return expectation, which Skirkanich defined as 6 to 8 percent above inflation and a return above the S&P 500 over a full market cycle. The frosting on the cake is to achieve these performance hurdles with less risk and volatility than the overall market. Fox is an excellent core or foundation manager. From this strong base, you can venture into more aggressive investment styles if you so desire.

At the end of 1991, another concern was the overvaluation of the largest, high-capitalization stocks in the S&P 500. According to Skirkanich, the valuations relative to the underlying fundamentals are out of kilter. For example, the highest 100 companies are selling at a multiple of 24 times. The average multiple historically has been 14 times. Additionally, these stocks normally sell at 1.5 times book value, yet today they sell at 2.7 times book value. These favorites among both individual and institutional investors are not candidates for Fox's portfolios. If Fox cannot purchase a company with an improving and better-than-average dividend yield, growing at 8 to 10 percent and selling at a 20 to 25 percent discount to the market, the firm will pass and maintain its client assets in cash.

After working in larger firms, Skirkanich never wants to become a megafirm, employing a staff of 50 or more people. Instead, he prefers to retain a small, tight-knit group of six to seven senior investment managers, plus assistants and an administrative staff. Skirkanich sees his firm potentially handling 300 to 400 clients, roughly double today's base, so that the qualitative and personal qualities do not get lost.

Being a history buff, Skirkanich remembers that an aggressive equity style works well in rapidly increasing (bull) markets, but it is the protection of client capital during the downturns that maintains client loyalty. During the interview he rattled off some recent sharp market decline examples including:

1. The Dow Jones Industrial Average 50 percent decline from peak in January 1973 to valley in December 1974.

2. The 10-day period in October 1987 when the S&P 500 dropped almost 35 percent, including a one-day drop of over 22 percent on October 19.

3. The Japanese market index, the Nikkei 225, which has plunged over 60 percent between December 1989 and April 1992.

From time to time, investors need to be reminded of what it takes in terms of percentage returns to offset an annual loss. As illustrated below, a 10 percent annual return goal results in a compounded two-year return of 21 percent. But if you lose 5 percent the first year, it takes a return of 27.4 percent the second year to get back on the 10 percent annual return track. It is obvious from this chart that the deeper the hole you dig in the first year, the more difficult it becomes to ever catch up. A 50 percent loss in the first year requires a 142 percent second year return—a highly unlikely event!

Return Objective (percent)	Year 1 Return (percent)	Needed Return in Year 2 (percent)	Two-Year Compounded Totals (percent)
+ 10.0%	+ 10.0%	+ 10.0%	+ 21.0%
+ 10.0	− 5.0	+ 27.4	+ 21.0
+ 10.0	− 10.0	+ 34.4	+ 21.0
+ 10.0	− 15.0	+ 42.4	+ 21.0

Return Objective (percent)	Year 1 Return (percent)	Needed Return in Year 2 (percent)	Two-Year Compounded Totals (percent)
+ 10.0	− 20.0	+ 51.3	+ 21.0
+ 10.0	− 25.0	+ 61.3	+ 21.0
+ 10.0	− 30.0	+ 72.5	+ 21.0
+ 10.0	− 35.0	+ 86.2	+ 21.0
+ 10.0	− 40.0	+ 101.7	+ 21.0
+ 10.0	− 50.0	+ 142.0	+ 21.0

Skirkanich is careful to point out that even with the use of his firm's strict valuation criteria and small staff, it is impossible to build a bulletproof portfolio. All you can do is shift the risk probability to your favor. Being a value manager requires a tremendous amount of patience, something most investors lack. It may take two to three years before the market rewards the value you have identified in a particular entity. In other words, his stocks don't increase in value overnight. The market always seems to wring out all but the true believers.

Fox Asset Management exhibits supreme confidence in its style and its ability to weather both good and bad times. Its discipline strips away most emotion, and the focus is on cash flow and the relative valuation between companies and other asset classes. Fox never allows itself to be carried away with the pop investment themes that dominate the financial press. This disciplined outlook plus the patience to be out of sync with the rest of the investment world has rewarded Fox's clients.

In the six short years since the firm's inception, Fox's clients have received better than market average rates of return with substantially less risk. Exhibit 7–3 shows Fox's rate of return versus the S&P 500 in bull, bear, and neutral markets. Under each scenario, Fox outperformed the averages. And knowing that your investment adviser's strategy has some rhyme and reason to it allows you to sleep well at night, which, in the investment world, is a rarity.

EXHIBIT 7–3
*Equity Management Report (December 1990) (Bull/Bear/Neutral
Analysis Equity Plus Cash)*

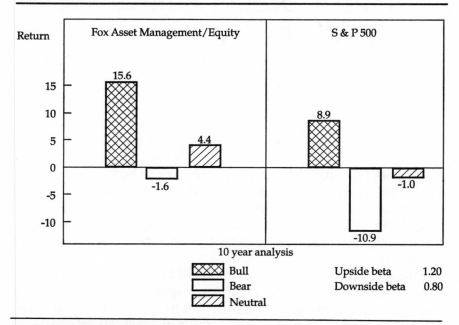

Chapter Eight

Harris Bretall Sullivan & Smith, Inc.
Investors in Successful U.S. Companies

What does Nike have in common with Home Depot? Amgen with Waste Management? Microsoft with Great Lakes Chemical? To the casual observer, almost nothing, except that all six are U.S.-based. But, to an investor, each represents the premier, best-managed organization in its particular industry, whether computers or tennis shoes.

These entities are what Harris Bretall Sullivan & Smith (HBSS) calls *successful companies*. By investing in quality growth companies *and* by preventing large losses (through the application of its asset allocation strategies of raising significant amounts of cash—75 percent—when the equity market became seriously overvalued), HBSS has placed in the top quartile of all investment managers for 1-, 3-, 5-, and 10-year periods ending December 31, 1991.

I. HISTORY AND PHILOSOPHY

David Harris, developer of the proprietary asset allocation and stock selection models and cofounder of HBSS, grew up in the small eastern Washington farming town of Omak, where he earned a football scholarship to the University of Idaho. A freak injury to his back forced him out of football and back to Central Washington College for an economics degree. After a stint in the navy from 1959–61, he landed an entry-level investment research position with Chicago-based Northern Trust. He was a specialist in the high technology area, which then included speculative companies such as Zenith, RCA, Texas Instruments, and Eastman Kodak. (My, has the world changed in 30 short years!)

With a slide rule and yellow pad, David Harris developed a crude version of what is one of today's most universally used stock valuation tools—the dividend discount model. He was once asked by the Northern Trust investment committee for his recommendation (buy, sell, or hold) for Eastman Kodak. Without a rationale or an answer for the committee, he used the Eastman Kodak projected dividend and growth rate to determine how long it would take investors to recapture their investment. To be consistent, he compared all the other so-called technology companies using the 3-month Treasury bill rates. From this analysis, he was able to rank all the companies in his high technology universe. Eastern Kodak fell toward the bottom of the list, thereby making it a sell candidate. This exercise was the beginning of what is now the Harris Bretall Sullivan & Smith investment success.

In 1971, Harris, after working in a number of investment positions (including managing Clark Dodge's investment arm in Chicago, directing research at a small Seattle brokerage firm, advising a mutual fund group of an insurance subsidiary and managing some offshore money for well-heeled investors from the Middle East and Europe), formed his own company along with Graeme Bretall and Howard McEldowny. Bretall, after graduating with a degree in finance from the University of Washington and gaining investment experience at J. P. Morgan in New York, managed the west coast research department for Kidder Peabody. A mutual friend of both men suggested the two get together because of their similar analytical approaches and investment philosophies. In discussing their similar investing backgrounds, Bretall stated, "Like myself, Dave had extensive experience in identifying and selecting successful quality companies. This dual experience, plus Dave's work in strategic asset allocation—raising significant cash when the equity markets became significantly overvalued—formed the core of the firm's investment philosophy."

Bretall introduced the view that it was possible to develop a universe of the 300 most successful companies. Based on his brokerage house research experience, he also believed that it was not possible to add value to the plethora of Street research on the well-known companies. He felt that their new firm *could* add value by identifying those lesser-known companies and concentrating the firm's research efforts on those companies. In discussing his firm's investment philosophy, Bretall stated, "The key to successful money management is to be able to create a portfolio of diversified stocks with strong fundamental characteristics. In order to do this, you need to employ a consistent and disciplined investment process."

In 1981, Jack Sullivan joined the firm as a principal. Sullivan, a chartered financial analyst, received his B.S. degree in accounting and his M.B.A. from Santa Clara University. In 1962, he entered the securities industry with Dean Witter & Co. He was a senior portfolio manager with the Bank of America in San Francisco from 1970 to 1973, where he participated in the design and implementation of the bank's investment counseling program. In 1973, Sullivan joined Western Asset Management Company as a manager of the San Francisco office. Here he met and hired Harry Smith, who was to join the firm in 1984. Sullivan brought to the firm not only his skills as an equity analyst, but his significant background in economics and the fixed-income markets.

In 1984, Western Asset's equity management group was merged with the firm, and Harry Smith joined as a principal, at which time Howard McEldowny retired. The firm name was changed to Harris Bretall Sullivan & Smith and became majority-owned by First Interstate Bank.

Harry Smith received his B.A. in political economics in 1972 from Colorado College. After graduation and prior to joining Western Asset Management Company, he worked at both Clark Dodge & Company and Kidder, Peabody & Company in San Francisco. He joined Western Asset's San Francisco office in 1975 as a senior portfolio manager. In 1981, he was promoted to manager of the San Francisco office and director of equity management; he also became a member of the equity strategy group and Western Asset's management committee.

HBSS's relationship with First Interstate was short lived, for, due to a significant change in the strategic direction of the bank, the principals took full ownership control of Harris Bretall Sullivan & Smith in 1987. The firm has followed the same team approach to research and investment decision-making for 20 years—surely a record in the industry.

EXHIBIT 8–1
Comparison of Performance Results

| | *Indata Equity Universe* | | | |
	10 YEARS 1982–1991	5 YEARS 1987–1991	3 YEARS 1989–1991	1 YEAR 1991
HBSS composite*	20.8%	20.4%	24.5%	49.3%
1st quartile	17.7	15.9	20.8	37.8
Median return	16.6	14.0	17.4	30.9
3rd quartile	15.0	12.6	14.8	26.4
S&P 500 Index	17.7	15.4	18.6	30.5

Database: Approximately 1,200 funds representing $168 billion.
Source: Indata Services Co.

| | *Indata Balanced Universe* | | | |
	10 YEARS 1982–1991	5 YEARS 1987–1991	3 YEARS 1989–1991	1 YEAR 1991
HBSS composite*	17.4	15.7	19.5	35.1
1st quartile	16.2	12.5	15.9	24.3
Median return	14.9	11.6	14.6	21.6
3rd quartile	14.4	10.7	13.3	19.3
S&P 500 Index	17.7	15.4	18.6	30.5

Database: Approximately 700 funds representing $33 billion.

Source: Indata Services Co.

* The Equity Return is calculated by using the returns of one of the firm's larger tax-exempt, discretionary equity accounts with $100 million in assets managed by HBSS over the 10-year period beginning 1981. The Balanced Return is calculated by using the returns of one of the firm's tax-exempt, discretionary balanced accounts with $5 million in assets managed by HBSS over the 10-year period beginning 1981. HBSS equity return represents equity portfolio plus cash equivalents, and both equity and balanced returns include reinvestment of all income. HBSS believes the results of its single longstanding client is, in each case, indicative of all of its clients' performance over the same period, but past results cannot and should not be used as an indicator of future performance and a single client's performance cannot and should not be used as an indicator of every client's future performance.

Net of management fees and commissions.

In describing the firm's teamwork, David Harris stated,

If you had known us for the past 20 plus years, the most remarkable part of our team is the friendship and camaraderie among the principals. The saying "One for all, all for one" describes our relation-

EXHIBIT 8–2
Investment Returns Since Inception (Yearly Percentage Gain or (Loss))

	Equity	Balanced	S&P 500	Lehman Bros G/C
1992	2.3	3.6	7.6	7.0
1991	49.3	35.1	30.5	16.1
1990	6.8	7.8	(3.2)	8.3
1989	20.9	17.1	31.7	14.2
1988	8.6	7.2	16.6	7.6
1987	21.1	13.2	5.3	2.3
1986	24.2	19.6	18.7	15.6
1985	31.5	26.3	31.8	21.3
1984	8.0	9.8	6.2	15.0
1983	17.3	13.3	22.5	7.9
1982	26.9	27.4	21.6	31.2
1981	(1.6)	1.7	(5.3)	7.2
1980	36.1	23.6	32.6	3.1
1979	34.4	21.6	18.5	2.3
1978	6.7	5.5	6.6	1.2
1977	(3.1)	0.1	(7.2)	2.9
1976	20.0	19.0	23.8	15.6
1975	18.1	16.2	37.1	12.3
1974	(11.4)	(8.2)	(26.5)	0.2
1973	(2.1)	(2.7)	(14.7)	2.3
1972	18.2	12.3	19.1	6.0

Harris Bretall Sullivan & Smith, Inc. computes performance using time-weighted total returns linked monthly, including accruals for interest and reinvestment of dividends and income. Portfolios within the composite are dollar-weighted and calculated after fees and commissions. In addition, the calculations are performed by our accounting system, Advent. The equity and balanced composites are built from all tax-exempt, fully discretionary accounts with opening balances of $3 million. Past results cannot and should not be used as an indicator of future performance.

ships. There is not one of us that won't pitch in and help, no matter if it's to hop a plane to make a presentation or handle a problem. This feeling permeates through the entire firm, which is one of the main reasons we've experienced such low turnover.

Although the principals value and emphasize their friendship, when it comes to economic interpretations, Federal Reserve policy, or investment decisions, the discussion can become quite heated. Their proprietary model and database provides them a focal point from which to argue. Basically, they ask, "What is wrong with what the model is telling us?" or even better, "What are we, the principals, missing?"

An overview of the results of the firm's investment process will clearly show its success. For a 20-year period, the HBSS equity portfolios have outperformed the S&P 500 by 3.6 percent average annual return, gross of fees but net of all commissions and transaction costs. At the same time, the firm's strategic asset allocation discipline has helped its clients avoid the bear markets of 1981–82, 1984, and 1987. Within the Indata measurement universe which tracks the actual portfolio performance of approximately 1,200 funds representing $168 billion, the HBSS equity and cash portfolios have ranked in the top decile (10 percent). The overall results are highlighted in Exhibit 8–1, while the year-by-year returns are listed in Exhibit 8–2.

II. STRATEGY

The entire HBSS investment process is graphically depicted in Exhibit 8–3, which highlights the firm's complex decision-making process. Each portion of this graph is explained in the following text.

A. *Economic Analysis and Investment Factors*

HBSS's decision-making process begins with a weekly investment meeting attended by the members of the strategy committee, which includes the four principals and the senior portfolio managers. Every Tuesday, the investment committee discusses the economic events, specific industry or company announcements, and investment factors which impact financial markets. The discussions begin with a review of the nine investment factors listed below. Each factor is reviewed and given a rating of positive (+), neutral (N), or negative (−):

1. Economy (recovery or recession).
2. Inflation (trend).
3. Interest rates (trend and momentum).

EXHIBIT 8–3
Investment Process

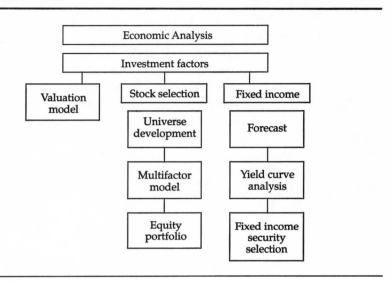

4. Earnings (trend and momentum).
5. Valuation/Volatility.
6. Federal Reserve policy (Fed and G-7).
7. Political environment.
8. International environment.
9. Supply and demand.

The object of this review is to look at the trend in each investment factor and determine what effect, if any, these trends will have on specific companies in its universe and the financial markets overall. The investment committee does not try to pin down the exact inflation or GNP figures—the committee is merely attempting to identify trends.

B. Strategic Asset Allocation

One of the key factors analyzed under the above section—stock market valuation—is used to make strategic asset allocation decisions. As described earlier, the firm has sidestepped most major

EXHIBIT 8–4
Valuation Model

A quantitative analysis of equity returns is implicit in the Harris Bretall asset allocation decision. Our valuation model takes the current interest rate yield on the 10-year U.S. Treasury note, long-term growth prospects for corporate profits, and our assumptions about current earnings and mathematically calculates the potential return available from equity investments. The market potential matrix below displays this procedure and indicates the level of attractiveness that stocks hold at current prices, under several different interest rate environments.

(A)	(B) (Add Risk Premium)	(C)	(D)	(E)	(F)	
			S&P 500 Earnings per Share		Percent Change From S&P at $410	
10-Year Note	Equity Target Return	Valuation P/E	1992 $23.00	1993 $26.00	1992	1993
6.0	7.0	20.5	471	533	13.1 %	23.1 %
6.5	7.5	18.6	428	484	4.3	15.3
7.0	8.0	17.1	394	445	(3.9)	8.0
7.5	8.5	15.6	358	405	(14.3)	(1.1)
8.0	9.0	14.3	329	372	(24.3)	(9.9)
8.5	9.5	13.2	304	344	(34.6)	(19.0)

stock market corrections through the disciplined application of the market potential matrix (Exhibit 8–4).

The theory behind the matrix is that the firm does not want to subject its clients to unnecessary risk when the stock market is excessively overvalued. Strategic asset allocation means raising significant amounts of cash (75 percent) at these times of serious overvaluation—which historically have happened once or twice a decade.

A step-by-step calculation in the matrix is as follows: first, HBSS compares the current interest rate environment in conjunction with the overall stock market. Using the 10-year U.S. Treasury note as a benchmark, HBSS determines investors should earn at least a 100 basis point return premium (1 percent) over a risk-free Treasury return. In this example, with the 10-year note currently paying 7.5 percent, the equity target return is 8.5 percent. This 8.5

percent is a minimum target rate of return. Thus, the lower the Treasury rate, the lower the equity target return.

Second, based on the stock market's historical trading patterns, the overall stock market is fairly valued at a price/earnings ratio of 15.6. For example, a 10 percent yield on Treasuries would equal a 10 price/earnings ratio.

Third, HBSS estimates the S&P 500 earnings for 1992 and 1993, which in the model are listed at $23 and $26, respectively. In calculating these figures, HBSS assumes an 8 percent long-term growth rate in earnings and a dividend payout ratio of 45 percent (45 percent of earnings are paid out in dividends to shareholders).

Finally, HBSS multiplies these S&P earnings projections by the P/E number to determine a fair valuation level for the S&P 500 in 1992 and 1993. Using the same example, the market is fairly valued at 373 for 1992 and 436 for 1993. Using the March 10, 1992, closing price of 404, today's market is overvalued by 8.1 percent for 1992 and 7.2 percent undervalued for 1993. Because the market is a discounting mechanism, HBSS looks at the market potential six to nine months out.

Are these figures worrisome for HBSS portfolio managers? As of September 1992, no! As long as the market ranges from undervalued to 25 percent overvalued, all portfolios are fully invested— meaning 95 to 100 percent of client capital is allocated to the HBSS-identified growth companies. If the valuation figures move to over 25 percent, then HBSS looks back to the economic and investment factors to determine if there is some compelling reason to stay fully invested. If not, portfolio holdings are gradually sold until the 75 percent cash position is reached. In reviewing this process, Harry Smith emphasized,

> One must remember that as important as valuation is for making key asset allocation decisions, it is only one of the eight economic factors. For us to reduce our position in stocks, we have to have a confirmation of overvaluation and a negative fundamental outlook. This is not something that suddenly appears, where one day we are bullish and the next bearish—it evolves over time.

When asked whether this model is being reviewed for change or modification, Harry flatly stated, "We dance with the lady who brought us to the party; we are not inclined toward changing partners."

In 1987, the overvaluation matrix first flashed a warning signal in the spring. By late spring, HBSS began reducing its equity exposure, and by summer, the equity exposure had been pared down to 25 percent. In Exhibit 8–5, the HBSS client equity exposure and reduction thereof are graphically highlighted. The S&P 500 is overlaid on the graph to visually demonstrate the effectiveness of these strategic asset allocation moves.

When does HBSS return its client portfolio to a 100 percent invested position? Once the market returns to within 10 percent of a fair-valued position, HBSS becomes fully invested. Interestingly, according to the HBSS model, the overall market has not reached a 20 percent undervalued level in HBSS's more than 20 years of operation.

C. Developing the Stock Candidate Universe

After analyzing the economic and investment factors and the overall market valuation, the next critical step for HBSS is to develop a universe of high-quality growth stocks. Using several on-line databases, HBSS screens approximately 5,000 publicly held companies for fundamental characteristics such as revenue growth, financial strength, market leadership, and management quality. Specifically, HBSS looks at the data as shown in Exhibit 8–6.

This qualitative, as well as quantitative, screening process results in a universe of 300 high-quality, growth-oriented stocks, with attractive fundamental characteristics and a minimum market capitalization of $1 billion. This review process is formally done twice a year and results in approximately 10 stocks being added and 10 being deleted. Exhibit 8–6 also compares the characteristics of the firm's universe with those of the S&P 500 index.

In the final analysis, HBSS has developed a stock universe from which to select 40 to 50 key stocks for inclusion in client portfolios. As with all the managers, the holdings in HBSS's portfolio will change significantly over time. HBSS was very complimentary of Arizonian Jerry Gould, who developed a database of 2,500 companies which HBSS uses to screen its stock universe. In describing the database, partner Jack Sullivan stated, "It was as if Jerry Gould had designed a system just for us. He took data from a variety of sources and reports and put it in one system. For example, we have the earnings estimates from 39 analysts covering

EXHIBIT 8–5
Strategic Asset Allocation

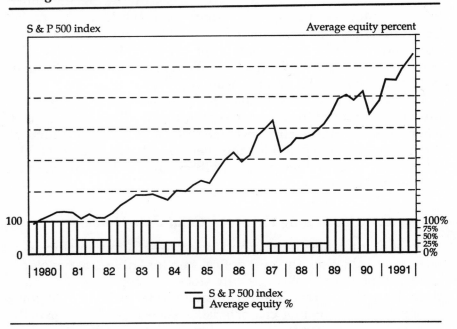

Microsoft in Gould's database. Gould's system, through graphics, has made the data much easier to analyze."

D.   Stock Selection

Armed with its 300 individual company stock universe, HBSS then turns its focus to the development of a model equity portfolio. Again, HBSS uses a proprietary model highlighted in Exhibit 8–7.
  There are four steps, along with their weightings, in the model.

  Step 1—present value model. First, companies are ranked based on their intrinsic present value, utilizing the HBSS earnings and growth rate outlook. Research responsibilities for industry sectors are as follows:

Capital goods, basic industry, technology   David Harris
Consumer sector   Graeme Bretall

EXHIBIT 8–6
Stock Universe Characteristics

	HBSS Universe	S&P 500
GROWTH		
5 years	8.9%	6.6%
10 years	11.3%	6.0%
Projected	13.0%	7.0%
PROFITABILITY		
ROE 5 years	19.0%	14.7%
Pretax margin	13.3%	7.4%
RISK		
P/E ratio	15.5x	16.5x
Debt ratio	25.0%	31.0%
Beta	1.1	1.0
DIVIDENDS		
Yield	2.2%	2.9%
Payout ratio	39%	59%
MARKET CAPITALIZATION		
Average	$8.5 billion	$22.2 billion

Source: Gould Research.

Energy, healthcare, media	Jack Sullivan
Interest-sensitive, transportation	Henry Smith

Together with the senior portfolio managers, the partners develop growth rates, earnings estimates, risk characteristics, and other variables for analysis. In applying the HBSS proprietary present value model, the following criteria are considered:

Growth rates.	Market volatility.
Financial strength.	Dividend payout.
Current stock price.	Present earnings outlook.
Earnings momentum.	Five-year earnings.
Market discount rate.	Earnings outlook confidence.

Using financial strength as an example, the HBSS analysis is clear. HBSS not only looks at the debt levels and ratings, but also at the

EXHIBIT 8–7
Model Portfolio Development

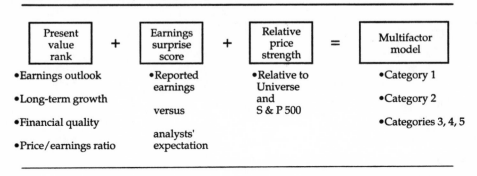

volatility and stability of earnings. All stocks are ranked from 1–5, with a 3 rating demonstrating average market characteristics (same as S&P 500). A better financial rating will move a stock up in the 300-stock universe rankings.

All of the above information is developed within the common economic framework which flows from HBSS's factor analysis. The analysts gather information on each company, primarily from Wall Street sources. Several databases are used to track actual changes in a company's balance sheet or income statement. It also is not unusual for company management to visit the firm's office in San Francisco or for individual company visits to take place out in the field. Given the limited number of companies in the model portfolio universe, HBSS is able to concentrate its resources and knows each company well.

While the companies in the firm's universe are intrinsically attractive companies at any given time, they may be undervalued or overvalued according to the multifactor model. The firm's stock selection process focuses on finding the best buy and sell points for each company. After extensive analysis, the model universe is ranked by fundamental attractiveness. Specifically, each stock's present value is compared to its current price, and the potential appreciation is calculated. These results are then stored in the model.

Step 2—trend in current earnings. Once a company's fundamental valuation is determined, the next step in the ranking process is to review its recent earnings success. Public companies spend a good deal of time counseling Wall Street analysts regarding their earnings projections. When reported earnings deviate from expected earnings, it is often a sign of a changing situation within the company or an inability to manage the change. The firm scores each company in the model portfolio universe through a rating system for its past quarterly earnings report. The range is +3 to −3, depending on the standard deviation of the earnings announcement. Reported earnings are adjusted for one-time events, such as write-offs or asset sales, before each company is scored. Therefore, HBSS is weighing only operating earnings. The adviser is especially wary of the "cockroach syndrome," whereby finding one bug under your bed means there are others lurking behind the furniture; one problem is often an indication of deeper problems within the company.

Step 3—price performance. The final part of the stock selection process is to rank each company by its price performance versus the S&P 500 and 300-stock universe. Basically, HBSS does not want to make a "dead money" mistake where a stock comes up as undervalued in step 1 but never appreciates in price. Like Avatar and Nicholas-Applegate, HBSS wants to see a stock price moving up. Harry Smith explained,

> The purpose of steps 2 and 3 is to make the dividend discount model more timely. The dividend discount model [step 1] continues to play the most dominant role in the stock selection because it identifies the most favorably priced (undervalued) companies. Unfortunately, undervalued stocks may stay undervalued for long periods of time, making the other two steps integral parts of the process.

Step 4—compiling the data from steps 1–3. Once this three-part review is completed, the entire model portfolio universe is ranked from top to bottom, combining the scores for each area to determine the most attractive companies in the model portfolio universe. The top 40–50 companies (category 1) are purchased for the model equity portfolio. Companies ranked in category 2 are "hold" stocks for the model equity portfolio, and companies ranked in categories 3, 4 and 5 are "sell" stocks for the model equity portfolio. Each security is dollar-weighted so that all company positions are equal. For example, the current HBSS 40-stock portfolio dictates that each company holds a 2.5 percent position. (At the publishing of this book, HBSS was strongly considering expanding their client portfolio holdings to the 50 most highly rated stocks. This will result in each stock holding a 2 percent portfolio position.) Stocks usually fall from the top two categories for four reasons:

1. They become very fundamentally overvalued due to rapid appreciation.
2. They have suffered changes in their long-term fundamentals (growth rates or earnings expectations).
3. They have announced a negative earnings surprise.
4. They have a negative price strength score that is not offset by attractive long-term valuation.

HBSS's process results in the model equity portfolio selling stocks that fall into categories 3, 4, or 5 and replacing them with stocks that rise into category 1. HBSS usually waits a few weeks before selling stocks once they drop into category 3. From time to time, a stock will temporarily move into category 3, only to go back to the safe grounds of categories 1 and 2. This is the process that results in a relatively low portfolio turnover of 40 to 50 percent per year (10 to 20 companies replaced and added). These stock sales and purchases usually occur following the quarterly earnings reports, resulting in three to four names being deleted and added. The average holding period for stocks is just over two years. Bretall provided this analogy in describing portfolio strategy:

> In order to be successful in this business you have to do two things. First, have the ability to identify attractive growth-oriented companies, and second, have the patience to hold them so their fundamentals will be reflected in the prices of the shares. It is a little like farming—you cannot be pulling the carrots out of the ground every other week to see if they are growing.

HBSS believes that if the model equity portfolio is followed, a client's money will be invested in the stocks which show the most appreciation potential. Interestingly, within an HBSS model

EXHIBIT 8–8
Multifactor Model Results (14-Year History, January 1, 1978 through December 31, 1991)

Portfolio	Cumulative Compound Period	Annualized Rate
S&P 500	719.70	16.21
Category 1*	1227.94	20.29
Category 2*	962.87	18.39
Category 3*	688.28	15.89
Category 4*	423.35	12.55
Category 5*	359.57	11.51
HBSS equity portfolios**	1185.43	20.01
HBSS universe*	749.19	16.51

* Gross of management fees and commissions.
** Net of management fees and commissions.

portfolio, 80 percent of the annual gains generally come from approximately 10 of the stocks. The other holdings range from above average to below average. And there is no way to predict the winners or average performers for the upcoming year—otherwise the job would be easy.

What HBSS has done is to take subjective judgments, like earnings projections, and systematize the data so that American Airlines can be compared to IBM. Does the HBSS model work? Exhibit 8–8 shows the actual results since January 1978. This table breaks the 300 stocks into categories, rebalances the returns monthly, and compares the results against the S&P 500. These results speak for themselves.

III.   SUMMARY

HBSS's average institutional client has been with the firm for close to 13 years, which indicates that HBSS is doing something right. Its disciplined investment process, which combines a strategic asset allocation model with a multifactor, three-part stock selection model, has given HBSS an edge among investment advisers. In discussing the stock selection model, David Harris stated, "Academic studies have shown that one can forecast 90 percent of a stock's movements if you can get a handle on the valuation, earnings momentum, and relative strength—and that's a full enough plate for us. We will leave the other 10 percent for someone else."

In addition to its equity portfolios, HBSS executes over $5 billion of fixed-income trades on an annual basis for a major institutional client. Although fixed-income performance has been exemplary, it is the equity management style that has bolstered the firm's reputation.

Over the past 20 years, HBSS's investment process has added approximately 3.8 percent over the S&P 500 with slightly less risk. Similar to other growth stock managers, you should expect higher volatility than the value-oriented managers. This can be especially noticeable when HBSS's strategic asset allocation model dictates a fully invested position in client portfolios. But growth stocks have temporarily fallen out of favor among the investment public. For this reason, HBSS is inappropriate for the faint of heart. For those growth-oriented investors who want to have their cake (i.e., obtain superior returns) and eat it too (have a manager who will attempt to sidestep the high risk periods), HBSS bears consideration.

Chapter Nine

Nicholas-Applegate Capital Management
Identifying and Capturing
Growth Worldwide

How does the cofounder and investment sage behind one of America's premier growth stock investment firms maintain a low profile? These days, for Art Nicholas, it is becoming difficult, if not impossible. His unique growth philosophy and its application have placed Nicholas-Applegate in the top 1 percent of all equity managers (see Exhibit 9–1). Along the way, he has developed a loyal and growing cadre of clients whose net worth has increased almost fivefold since 1980—a track record second to none.

With over $8 billion under management, Nicholas-Applegate applies the same stock selection disciplines in its minicapitalization (under $100 million), emerging growth/small capitalization ($100–500 million), middle capitalization ($500 million–$5 billion), international/global, convertible, balanced, and hedged portfolios.

Whether selecting a small- or medium-sized company in the United States or in the foreign markets, the Nicholas-Applegate portfolio managers focus on the same four key elements:

1. Earnings acceleration.
2. Sustainable growth.
3. Positive relative price strength.
4. Valuation.

EXHIBIT 9–1
Nicholas-Applegate's Long-Term Results and Rankings (Total Returns over 7.0 Years from January 1, 1985 through December 31, 1991)

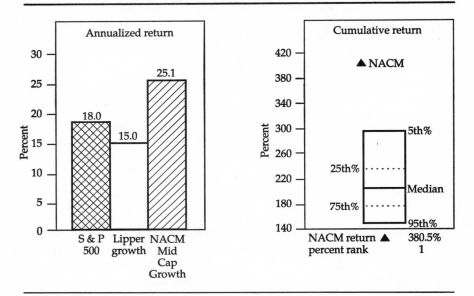

Source: SEI Corporation.

I. HISTORY

Before forming Nicholas-Applegate in August 1984, Art Nicholas first applied his growth philosophy and strategies at San Diego Trust & Savings Bank in 1977. Later, he became the chief investment officer at Pacific Century Group, a subsidiary of Security Pacific Bank, where he teamed up with Fred Applegate. In August 1989, the two left the bank to set up their own shop, and, as a credit to their reputation and trust, Nicholas-Applegate's three largest clients faithfully followed.

The initial $40 million under management quickly grew to almost $100 million in the first 12 months with the addition of their first major corporate client, Eli Lilly & Co. Armed with Nicholas's number one ranking among almost 300 bank-managed funds for 1982 and 1983, Applegate applied his excellent marketing skills and told the pension world their growth stock story.

Since 1984, Nicholas-Applegate has grown rapidly, now employing 30 professional portfolio and client service managers in managing over $8 billion; it has over 75 support persons. Unlike many investment firms, Nicholas-Applegate separates the client service and portfolio functions. Although separate, each division maintains the same status level within the organizational hierarchy. This system differentiates Nicholas-Applegate from some advisory firms which view the client servicing function as a notch below the portfolio management function. As Eileen Delasandro, partner and director of client service/marketing, commented, "Most clients prefer to have their portfolio managers 100 percent focused on managing their money, not traveling around the country. Additionally, a portfolio manager may not be the best communicator or servicer of client needs; therefore, allowing each function to concentrate on its area of expertise has been positively received and accepted by our clients." Nicholas-Applegate's active trading style requires that its portfolio managers remain anchored to their posts from 5:30 A.M. to the market close each day, rather than attempt to manage their portfolios from an airport. This unique organizational structure allows Nicholas-Applegate to align portfolio responsibilities along market, risk, and company capitalization mandates and segments. Instead of managing 30 to 40 client relationships, for example, a portfolio manager working in the international markets is responsible for all investments in that segment.

Following Nicholas's lead, all the professionals are focused on beating the market and serving their clients. Placing in the top 20 percent is not good enough; they seek the top 1 percent performance. Its professionals come to Nicholas-Applegate with varied educational and economic backgrounds, but they share a demonstrated success in their past careers and carry this attitude to their jobs. As consultant and board member Fred Applegate explained, "We like to take young, successful people from completely different backgrounds with five to seven years' experience and train them in the Nicholas-Applegate investment philosophy." The varied education and family backgrounds creates an intellectually challenging environment in which each employee is encouraged to excel.

The Nicholas-Applegate client list ranges from the prestigious endowment funds of Stanford and Yale University to America's largest corporations, unions, and local and state employee funds. In addition, to allow access for the small investor, Nicholas-Applegate initiated an open-ended mutual fund which was up 55.5 percent in 1991. Managed by portfolio professional Jack C. Marshall, this fund concentrates on only middle capitalization ($500 million to $5 billion in size) companies. Again, the same investment philosophy, principles, strategies, and stock selection disciplines are strictly adhered to by Marshall in managing the Nicholas-Applegate growth equity fund.

II. PHILOSOPHY

Although Art Nicholas shuns the publicity and emphasis placed on his role in the firm, Robert E. Anslow, international portfolio manager and the developer of Nicholas-Applegate's esteemed proprietary quantitative system, flatly stated, "The investment philosophy and portfolio strategies from which we developed our stock selection system came directly from the artificial network of Art Nicholas's brain." Nicholas-Applegate has taken what began as a small capitalization/emerging growth strategy and expanded it into a high-technology, systematized approach for all market segments.

Art Nicholas, trying to play down the success of the Nicholas-Applegate model, stated, "I had no grand scheme when I first started managing money. There are all kinds of ways to make money in the markets. I just felt more comfortable in stocks that were moving and having my investment confirmed by the market versus buying an undervalued asset and waiting for it to turn around." Nicholas-Applegate believes one needs to look at companies "at the margin." These changes at the margin, for example earnings growth and acceleration, provide a sign of sustainability of growth and a precursor for improving company fundamentals. The Nicholas-Applegate philosophy can be best summed up as follows: "Over time the market rewards those companies that are demonstrating rapid earnings growth, and we at Nicholas-Applegate believe we have developed the best investment selection process to identify potential market winners."

III. STRATEGY

To understand Nicholas-Applegate's investment strategy, first learn what they profess *not* to do. Nicholas-Applegate has little interest in the economy, the Federal Reserve's position, or the technical condition of the overall stock and bond markets. Moreover, Nicholas-Applegate's portfolio managers do not attempt to "time the market" (making large shifts of money in and out of the stock market depending on whether the company is bullish, neutral, or bearish on the market's prospects over the next three to six months). In reviewing Nicholas-Applegate's position on market timing, Bob Anslow commented,

> There is no evidence that profitable market timing can be done on a consistent basis. But there is sufficient evidence to suggest that market timing involves extreme risk of being out of the market at the wrong time. We neutralize the stock market and risk through expert stock selection, not trying to make big bets on the stock market's next big move up or down.

In backing Nicholas-Applegate's position on market timing, client service and marketing representative Mark J. Correnti cited the Datastream, University of Michigan, Ibbotson Associates, and Sanford C. Bernstein & Company studies which statistically cover the years 1980 through 1989. During the bull market running 1982 through 1987, an investor who had left his money fully invested in the S&P 500 for all 1,276 trading days would have receivd a 26.3 percent annualized rate of return. Had the investor been out of the market and in U.S. Treasury bills for the 40 best days of 1,276 trading days, the portfolio rate of return would have dropped to a meager 4.3 percent, less than that of U.S. Treasury bills. Had the investor missed the 30 best days, he would have earned 8.5 percent per year; the 20 biggest days, 13.1 percent per year; and the 10 best gaining days, 18.3 percent per year. Exhibit 9–2 includes the last 20 years stretching from 1972 through 1991. The results tell the same story—being out of the market for even short periods can substantially reduce investor returns.

The outstanding stock market returns of 1991 reinforced the perils of market timing. The 30 percent or more returns the stock market offered in 1991 were garnered during the first 10 days following the inception of the Iraq war and the last 10 business

EXHIBIT 9–2
Market Timing

	S&P 500	
1972–1991	*Cumulative Return (percent)*	*Annualized Return (percent)*
Entire 20 years	846.1%	11.8%
Minus 1 best month (0.4% of the time)	711.6	11.0
Minus 3 best months (1.3% of the time)	535.1	9.6
Minus 5 best months (2.1% of the time)	404.0	8.4
Minus 10 best months (4.2% of the time)	200.1	5.6

Source: Kidder, Peabody & Company.

days of the year. During the time sandwiched between these two 10-day periods (the other 48 weeks), the market just tread water. For 1991, there were more down days than up days. Had you missed these 10 key up days, you would have had a negative rate of return in a year whereas Nicholas-Applegate's growth portfolios achieved over 50 percent rates of return.

The Nicholas-Applegate stock selection process as outlined in Exhibit 9–3 begins with a quantitative ranking of over 3,500 stocks on the basis of 16 key variables that can be broadly grouped into four key screen filters.

A. Earnings Acceleration

Here Nicholas-Applegate is looking for one to two quarters of positive earnings surprises and momentum due to new, innovative products or services, changes in the economic, competitive, or regulatory environment, or a different management approach. Especially attractive are companies whose reported earnings are much higher than analysts' estimates and where analysts' estimates are being revised upward. Nicholas-Applegate has found earnings acceleration to be an early indication of sustainable earnings patterns.

EXHIBIT 9-3
The Investment Process Is Disciplined and Thorough

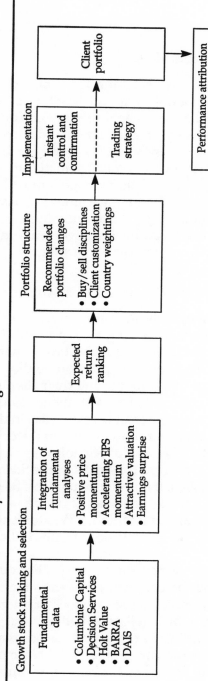

B. Sustainable Growth

Nicholas-Applegate is searching for companies that will sustain the earnings acceleration for at least two to three quarters. However, portfolio managers are wary of companies that show big earnings gains by balance sheet and income statement manipulation. To be a candidate for purchase in client portfolios, a company must demonstrate something unique; then the Nicholas-Applegate portfolio managers must have a high degree of confidence that the dramatic earnings increase will continue. As Art Nicholas commented, "We are not interested solely in growth per se; instead we focus on improvements in growth as represented by unexpected increase in earnings."

C. Positive Relative Price Momentum

Nicholas-Applegate only invests in stocks of companies that are moving up and are exhibiting strong positive price momentum relative to their industries and the broad market averages. The portfolio managers attempt to position holdings with little institutional ownership, therefore placing their clients' funds in front of an institutional buying wave. With institutions being the biggest market players, a small percentage increase in their ownership can provide a substantial lift to the individual stock prices. The average institutional ownership of Nicholas-Applegate holdings is 37 percent versus 50 percent for stocks in the S&P 500. In the emerging growth portfolios, it is under 20 percent. Its portfolio managers will quickly sell a stock that is not showing favorable price movement. Jack Marshall commented, "We don't want 'dead money' [fine companies with reasonable earnings but are failing to appreciate in value]."

Bob Anslow confirmed the strategy: "For our portfolios to perform in the upper percentiles, we need to make timely purchases of our stocks. We need to see the stock of interest outperform the general market, which tells us that the rest of the investment community is starting to recognize the positive aspects we identified with the particular company." This momentum confirms that a particular company's business is improving. Price momentum is an excellent risk-adjusted predictor of price persistence.

D. *Valuation*

Nicholas-Applegate closely reviews and updates growth companies' free cash flow from operations and return on investment figures. Its portfolio managers not only review the current figures but also calculate the rate of change in the free cash flow numbers and how the changing earnings stream will impact that entity's free cash flow and return on investment figures. By removing all accounting distortions, placing all companies in the same ballpark by measuring actual cash flow performance, and determining the true economic value of each company, Nicholas-Applegate's portfolio managers can set a price at which they are willing to buy or sell an individual security.

The relative weightings of these four key variables change over time from quarter to quarter. Just as relative strength analysis is used for stock selection, Nicholas-Applegate applies the same discipline in modifying its four screening filters; those variables providing the best predictive value for stock price gains for the last four quarters receive the heavier weightings. The 3,000 to 3,500 stocks are ranked on the basis of the four key characteristics. Usually only the top 15 percent are considered for purchase and are quickly disposed of if their individual ranking drops below 40 percent, unless there is some dramatic positive change occurring within the company or its competitive environment. The top 300 (15 percent) ranked companies are screened to identify the best 40 to 60 stocks for client portfolios. With Nicholas-Applegate growing so rapidly, liquidity risk (being able to easily move in or out of a stock without disrupting the price) is a growing concern. Ashley Rabun commented, "The last thing we want is to try to turn the Queen Mary around in a small pond." To limit this risk, Nicholas-Applegate limits its holdings to no more than 5 percent of the outstanding stock of any one company. As a general rule of thumb, the firm avoids owning more than three to five days' trading volume in one stock. Additionally, Nicholas-Applegate sets a cap on how much money it will accept within one market segment. This is especially critical in the small capitalization market where liquidity risk can be high. Finally, this liquidity risk is neutralized by Nicholas-Applegate's trading expertise. The head trader has been with the firm since its inception. The firm has developed considerable expertise in maneuvering in and out of the over-the-counter market. Steve McNally, vice president and portfolio manager, commented, "An investor has no business participating and trading in these markets without considerable experience and history in these arenas."

The investment adviser's portfolio managers are quick to point out that their success is not because of a mechanical, strictly systematized, "black box" model. As Catherine Avery said, "Yes, we are quantitatively oriented, but our system is very pragmatic—you don't see a lot of eggheads making portfolio decisions around here."

The human side to decision-making at Nicholas-Applegate begins with its close relationship with an extensive network of analysts, brokerage houses, and developers of outside databases. Beginning when Art Nicholas was with Security Pacific over 15 years ago and continuing today with all the portfolio managers, Nicholas-Applegate has initiated and maintained close relationships with the best minds on Wall Street. Basically, these research analysts bring Nicholas-Applegate exceptional growth stock ideas from which its portfolio managers can pick and choose. No idea is overlooked or rejected. When an idea is brought up to a Nicholas-Applegate manager from the external environment, the portfolio manager can review and compare any information received to the data generated from the internal quantitative system within a few minutes. The biggest winning ideas have come from regional brokerage analysts who can look in their own backyards. Nicholas-Applegate portfolio managers have developed a trust with over 75 of these geographically dispersed research analysts and traders. The company rewards their research ideas by directed trading. Jack Marshall commented,

> We are very specific on the type of companies we want for our client portfolios—companies that are growing "geometrically" but have little institutional ownership. We are very hard on external research analysts. They know exactly what type of ideas we are looking for, and we want to own them before the rest on the street. The end results are portfolios of companies growing at 25 to 100 percent annually versus a market average of 3 to 5 percent.

Art Nicholas speculates that 80 percent of the firm's portfolio positions came from ideas generated in its external environment. Their telephones ring nonstop from 5 A.M. PDT until after the markets close at 7 P.M. PDT. It is not unusual for Nicholas-

Applegate's portfolio manager to receive up to 40 calls an hour from brokerage analysts. What distinguishes Nicholas-Applegate from other investment firms is the integration of the external growth ideas with its quantitative system (Exhibit 9–4). The adviser employs no internal research analysts because, in its view, research analysts are only as good as their last few money-making ideas. Therefore, Nicholas-Applegate is not put in the position of firing employees if their ideas do not pan out. The firm's portfolio managers take the externally generated ideas and cross-check their quantitative system of inputs.

Nicholas-Applegate has opened its pocketbooks when it comes to investing in the latest technology. If they mean an investment edge, few acquisitions or upgrades are questioned. As a tribute to Nicholas-Applegate's technological systems, $1.5 to 2 million is spent annually. With two microvax computers operating 24 hours a day through which all stocks are reranked weekly, the adviser checks out the stock ideas against the earnings, momentum, relative strength, and valuation criteria. The quantitative system provides a safety net to ensure that that methodology is consistently applied. In discussing this blend of quantitative and external research, Bob Anslow stated,

> The two systems complement each other, and the client portfolios perform better than if you used one system on its own. Occasionally, external analysts become too emotional, and therefore their objective view is tainted. In addition, there are times when our growth style is out of favor on Wall Street [the external network is preaching the value of cyclical stocks]. Rather than follow the herd, the quantitative system rejects all the ideas and reminds us to stick to our discipline.

Many times, the external network will identify changes at the margin before they are picked up by the numbers in the internal system.

Consistent with its buy philosophy and strategy, stocks are sold under six scenarios:

1. Earnings momentum and growth have slowed or flattened.
2. Earnings stability becomes questionable.
3. The valuation (stock) becomes too rich.
4. The stock price or the industry as a whole demonstrates poor relative strength.
5. A better candidate is identified, therefore precipitating a replacement for the stock in question.

EXHIBIT 9–4
Superior Relative Equity Performance

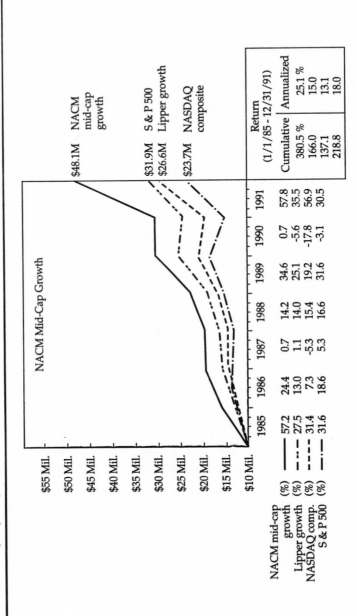

		1985	1986	1987	1988	1989	1990	1991
NACM mid-cap growth	(%)	57.2	24.4	0.7	14.2	34.6	0.7	57.8
Lipper growth	(%)	27.5	13.0	1.1	14.0	25.1	-5.6	35.5
NASDAQ comp.	(%)	31.4	7.3	-5.3	15.4	19.2	-17.8	56.9
S & P 500	(%)	31.6	18.6	5.3	16.6	31.6	-3.1	30.5

NACM Mid-Cap Growth

$48.1M   NACM mid-cap growth

$31.9M   S & P 500
$26.6M   Lipper growth

$23.7M   NASDAQ composite

	Return (1/1/85 – 12/31/91)	
	Cumulative	Annualized
	380.5 %	25.1 %
	166.0	15.0
	137.1	13.1
	218.8	18.0

6. The variables behind the dramatic earnings and price explosion no longer exist or have changed.

All buys and sells are made by the individual portfolio managers who are assigned responsibility for a specific investment mandate. There are no once-a-week investment strategy meetings or formal committee approaches. Nor are Nicholas-Applegate's portfolio managers cloistered in private corner offices. Instead, decisions are made in a wide open, 40-by-40-foot war room which is highly conducive to constant, minute-by-minute communication among the portfolio managers, traders, and external research sources.

The trigger to buy and sell is made instantaneously. Nicholas-Applegate limits its portfolio holdings to 40 to 60 issues at one time, and turnover averages almost 100 percent annually. In explaining its active style, client service representative Brad Schluter commented, "Two thirds of the portfolio is held for one year or longer. In searching for stocks we want to hold, the other one third is turned over two and a half to three times per year. If a better idea comes along, one of the core portfolio stocks is bumped out." Unlike most value managers, stocks are never removed from its client portfolio because of price appreciation. Nicholas-Applegate never wants to discount the potential growth and price appreciation of a fast-growing company. In other words, the firm never knows how good the future could be. Had it applied strict value screens, companies such as Home Depot and Wal-Mart would have been sold at less than half of their current values. Again, this is part of the company's discipline—concentration on a few growth stocks that meet its strict criteria.

IV. SUMMARY

In 1990, the esteemed institutional and corporate publication *Pension & Investments* identified the "Magnificent 7" money managers of the 1980s. At the top of the list in terms of performance was equity manager Nicholas-Applegate (see Exhibit 9–4). For the last three years, ending December 31, 1992, Nicholas-Applegate's team of aggressive portfolio managers has beaten nearly every market index. The emerging growth account has outperformed the Wilshire Associates small company growth index by almost 12 percent (24.44 percent versus 12.84 percent). The midcap and convertible accounts are not far behind, each beating their comparative indices by between 9 and 10 percent.

The Nicholas-Applegate portfolio managers concentrate on smaller- to medium-sized companies with geometrically accelerating earnings caused by a specific event or situation, or institutional ownership and price momentum. The firm values the stock by measuring net cash flow to ensure it is not paying too much for the company's future growth.

Where does a firm like Nicholas-Applegate belong in a client's portfolio? Due to the volatility of the markets within its portfolio managers' work, the firm's style is not for the weak-kneed individual susceptible to panic attacks. Nicholas-Applegate is likened to a high-performance European road machine featuring both the latest and best automobile technology. For a person with a longer-term time horizon and an aggressive growth posture, Nicholas-Applegate cannot be beat.

In 1991, Nicholas-Applegate's portfolios were up over 50 percent, but during the overall market correction of 1992, Nicholas-Applegate was down approximately 10 percent through the first eight months. But even though the broad market has declined, Nicholas-Applegate's portfolio managers are not overly concerned as long as they can identify and purchase stocks which are either meeting or exceeding Wall Street's earnings estimates. In fact, broad market declines are welcomed by the firm's portfolio team as it allows the purchase of favorite securities at much more attractive prices. For example, for the first two quarters of 1992, the Hambrecht and Quist Growth Index declined over 25 percent, while 36 of the 40 Nicholas-Applegate mid-capitalization portfolio holdings reported at- or above-consensus earnings projections. As long as companies' growth remains strong, the adviser worries little about the short-term gyrations of the market.

What makes Nicholas-Applegate successful? It is the active overlay and interplay among the external data sources, the state-of-the-art internal system, and the portfolio manager trading expertise. Using what is called its *systems plus* network, Nicholas-Applegate has developed an elaborate sensing structure that allows its portfolio managers and traders to pick up even the slightest of changes in a company's fundamentals or its competitive environment. What comes to mind is an octopus with its many tentacles picking up any or all information and then quickly transmitting this information to the body, which includes the artificial intelligence and portfolio management expertise.

How does one summarize Nicholas-Applegate's elaborate and complex strategy? Initially, Nicholas-Applegate's portfolio managers are looking for some type of a change (positive or negative) in a company's earnings reports or trends, insider buying, industry dynamics, management, long-term product decline, and/or relative price momentum. Then they determine whether this change is sustainable by fundamental analysis, seeking contrasting views through their external network and confirming the new information through their internal quantitative system. Finally, they ask themselves, is the idea timely? Nicholas-Applegate wants to recognize the idea early versus the consensus on Wall Street, see some relative strength acceleration, and make sure the idea is so attractive that it warrants the replacement of a current holding.

What are growth areas for Nicholas-Applegate? First, its expert stock-picking system lends itself well to the hedge area, in which the most attractive stocks (top 10 percent rankings) are purchased, and the least attractive (lower 10 percent of the quantitative system) are sold short. This creates a market-neutral position which concentrates on stock selection—Nicholas-Applegate's specialty.

Additionally, institutions and individuals needing to bolster their rates of return are allocating additional funds to and looking for portfolio services for the small- to medium-sized company arena. Historically, growth stocks have outperformed other classifications of equities during slow growth environments, as expected in the 1990s.

The most promise lies in the opening up of international markets, which should prove to be fertile hunting grounds for the firm's definitive style. In the last year, Nicholas-Applegate has entered into several joint research ventures to take information on foreign stocks and neutralize their inherent taxation and accounting differences so that they can be compared to U.S. stocks. The end product will be a portfolio of the best 40 to 60 growth stocks from countries throughout the world. Once the systems are fully developed, Nicholas-Applegate will have a decisive investment edge over other investment advisers attempting to invest worldwide with crude and less-developed technology. Accelerated but disciplined growth seems to be the watchword for both Nicholas-Applegate and its clients' portfolios.

Chapter Ten

Regent Investor Services

"The name of the game is rotation."

Minnesota Fats

Regent Investor Services (RIS) has three core beliefs which drive its investment philosophy, discipline, strategy, and tactics:

1. Preservation of capital. Preserving capital during periods of market adversity, low volatility, and performance consistency are paramount objectives at RIS. Harold W. Stein, senior vice president and lead portfolio manager, summed up this objective with, "A missed market opportunity is less regrettable than a loss of capital."

Regent believes you have two choices as a money manager and/or investor:

1. You can shoot for being the number one manager in the country in terms of performance, which means you'll either see your picture on the front of *Barron's* or you'll "flare out," taking your client capital down with you.
2. You can aim for a consistent, low volatility record where you may not be number one in absolute terms, but you rank near the top in terms of risk-adjusted rates of return.

RIS prefers the second avenue. Quoting from Will Rogers, RIS CEO Michael Delfino stated, "I'm not as concerned with the return on my money as the return of my money." RIS uses a "belt and suspenders" investment style where, over the long term, the returns place it in the top 20 percent of all money managers, but it subjected its clients to 40 percent less risk than the overall markets.

 2. Big picture focus. Understanding the political, economic, and social trends and their impact on the various market
sectors and industries is more important than individual company
fundamentals. RIS investment strategy group and portfolio managers would rather own the worst stock in the best performing
sector than the best stock in the worst performing sector. (A sector
is a group of stocks in a particular industry, such as oil or airlines.)
Kenneth Safian, RIS investment strategist and director, explained,

> There is a time to own auto stocks and there is a time not to own them.
> The relative attractiveness of different industries and sectors changes
> frequently. By utilizing a "big picture" approach, we first try to iden-
> tify the key economic, political, and social trends and then, based on
> our outlook, we attempt to identify which sectors and industries will
> benefit and which will suffer from these trends. Finally, we over-
> weight and underweight our portfolios in those industries and sectors
> that fit our outlook.

Delfino added, "Most investment advisers and individual investors spend 80 percent of their time and effort studying individual
company fundamentals and 20 percent of their time analyzing the
economic, political, and social shifts. We do the exact opposite."
In Exhibit 10–1, the importance of this reverse analysis—focusing
on the market and sector/industry groups—is illustrated.

As shown on the left side of Exhibit 10–1, only 20 percent of a
stock's price movement comes from its specific fundamentals,
how well the company is managed, the return on equity, or its
financial condition. The other 80 percent comes from factors unrelated to a specific company: 31 percent is market-related, and 49
percent is directly related to the performance of the company's
sector or industry group. On the right side of the chart is the
typical investment adviser's focus in which 80 percent is centered
on company fundamentals, 10 percent on the stock market as a
whole, and 10 percent on the sector/industry groups. RIS believes
that no one sector, industry, or approach provides favorable absolute returns in all market cycles; therefore, portfolios must be
continually adjusted accordingly. Investing in the right sector is
critical for generating outstanding portfolio performance. As depicted in Exhibit 10–2, while growth stocks provided the best

EXHIBIT 10–1
Regent Sector Approach (The Critical Difference)

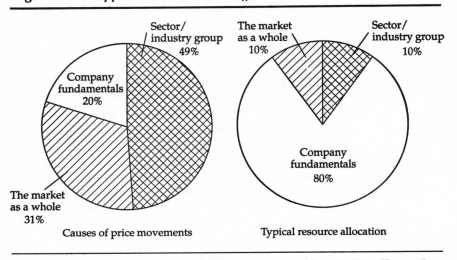

Causes of price movements   Typical resource allocation

Source: King, Benjamin F. "The Latent Statistical Structure of Security Price Changes".
Data from: Hagin, Robert and Mader, Chris, *What Today's Investor Should Know about:
THE NEW SCIENCE OF INVESTING* (Homewood, Ill.: Dow Jones-Irwin, 1973), pp. 90–93.

returns in 1977–83 and 1988–91, this sector underperformed the value sectors in the time periods 1972–77 and 1983–88.

3. No permanent safe havens for capital. Consistent with its sector rotation focus, RIS believes the old Wall Street "buy and hold forever" adage does not work anymore. RIS feels that it must actively manage its client portfolios, continually rotating funds from those that are overvalued to those that are not only relatively undervalued, but that offer the best growth opportunities as identified in the sector analysis. In describing the importance of maintaining a flexible stance, James E. Brady, senior vice president and director of marketing, stated, "In 1962, 30 years ago, had you purchased a 30-year Treasury bond, you would have earned a 4 percent annual interest rate plus receive your original capital back. But along the way, you would have suffered a devastating loss of purchasing power. In 1962, $10,000 would have bought you a nice house. Today, you may be able to purchase an expensive subcompact automobile."

EXHIBIT 10–2
Growth versus Value (1972–1991)

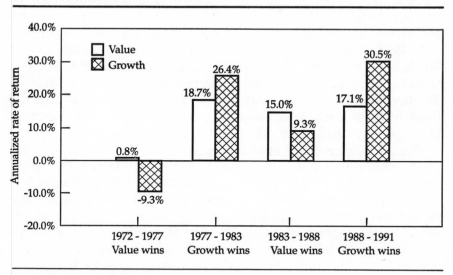

Source: Wilshire Capital Market.

I.   HISTORY AND PHILOSOPHY— TOP-DOWN SECTOR ROTATOR WITH A THEMATIC APPROACH

Regent Investor Services is an investment counseling subsidiary of Shields Asset Management. Although both RIS and Shields follow the same investment philosophy and strategies, the RIS arm was formed to handle individual, endowment, and small institutional funds, while Shields concentrates its efforts on larger institutional clients such as public funds and jointly administered labor-management plans. Shields, with over $6 billion under management, is one of the leading providers of investment services for organized labor plans.

Shields Asset Management, Inc. was formed in 1975 by Richard Nolan and James Dunseith as the pension fund investment management of Bache, Halsey, Stuart, Shields (which later became part of Prudential Securities). The investment department operated under the name Shields Capital Management. Jay Carr, a managing director at The Harbor Group, and Wilfred Lumer, who worked for another pension management firm, joined forces with Dunseith and Nolan. Together, they severed their ties with the brokerage firm to become an independent investment manager.

In 1978, Maurice Mandel, also from The Harbor Group, joined Shields, followed by the last principal and current CEO, Michael Delfino, in 1982. Delfino had competed head-to-head against Shields Asset Management as the head of trust operations for the Bank of New York, Westchester County Division, and therefore knew the firm and its principals.

The professional RIS staff has expanded over the years to include Kenneth Safian, investment strategist; Harold W. Stein, senior vice president; Deborah Grossman, portfolio manager; Salvatore Tartaglione, portfolio manager; Robert C. Ringstad, vice president-operations; James E. Brady, senior vice president-director of marketing; James F. Lyons, CFP, vice president-western region; Bill C. Taylor, vice president-south central region; Jay Tyler, vice president-eastern division; Angelo Barr, vice president-midwest division; and Robert M. Ohanesian, vice president-director of fixed-income investments. The average RIS professional has spent 8 years with the firm and 16 years in the industry.

In June 1988, Xerox Financial Services, through another highly regarded investment counseling subsidiary, Furman Selz, purchased Shields Asset Management and Regent Investor Services. RIS has the financial support of its well-capitalized parent, but is allowed to operate independently.

Regent and Shields operate independently as investment counseling affiliates with headquarters located in White Plains, New York, and regional representatives in Arlington, Texas; Boulder, Colorado; Southport, Connecticut; and Newport Beach and San Francisco, California.

What separates RIS from other conservative, top-down investment advisers? Safian summed up what makes RIS's research distinguishable from its competitors with,

> Most money managers do pursue common goals and objectives. We all search for value. We all want growth. What may differentiate firms such as ours is the consistency of the application of an established

discipline. We have created, over the years, a proprietary database of economic indicators which has proven effective in giving us a unique insight to trends developing in the market. It is the interpretation of our key indicators by seasoned professionals that creates our value and separates us from our competitors.

RIS's strength lies in its economic analysis and study of pertinent economic, political, and fundamental factors. This analysis leads the firm to judgments on market and sector trends. These judgments, in turn, allow the RIS investment strategy group portfolio managers to formulate guidelines for weighting client portfolios by sector and industry groups.

How was the firm's conservative investment philosophy developed? Delfino explained, "Our philosophy evolved to meet the conservative nature of our founding client base, multiemployer plans. With collective bargaining agreements, there is a focus on preservation of capital. We developed, out of necessity, the strong understanding of the importance of avoiding loss of capital, yet providing competitive returns." This philosophy is especially important when one views changes in the work environment where union membership and contributions continue to fall, yet demands on the plans are rising. RIS found that this orientation toward capital preservation and performance consistency naturally translated to the needs of individual, institutional, and corporate investors as well.

To assist the founding partners in facilitating the conservative needs of its client base, RIS and Shields brought in expertise in the area of economic and sector analysis. Smilen and Safian, a firm responsible for the *dual market principle,* which identified the divergence between growth and cyclical stocks, became the major provider of research and strategy for the firm. Ken Safian, RIS chief investment strategist, is widely recognized in the investment management field for having introduced the second major theory of sectoralization of the stock market nearly 25 years ago (the first was the *Dow theory,* propounded by Charles Dow in the late 1800s). Safian's segmentation of the stock market into growth and cyclical sectors has been hailed as a significant modern advance. The combination of Safian's work and RIS's basic philosophy tenets has provided an excellent framework from which to manage conservative client funds.

II.   EQUITY STRATEGY—IDENTIFYING AND OVERWEIGHTING FAVORABLE SECTORS

Rather than relying on a market timing approach, RIS concentrates on analyzing the economy and markets on a sectoral and group basis. RIS has divided the market into 6 sectors, 21 subsectors, and 65 industry groups. To measure the health of the economy, Safian and RIS have developed 23 different measures or series representing the major segments of business activity—financial, monetary, macroeconomic, labor, and consumer attitudes. Their investment strategy is developed through the continuous analysis of economic, political, and fundamental trends which influence the market as a whole and its sectors. A proprietary database of over 1,000 economic indicators has been developed from the 30 years of Safian's experience. On two-by-four-foot charts, Safian has traded and registered key economic data for over 30 years. RIS's top-down approach provides the backbone for further study of the equity and fixed-income markets and the opportunities within their sector and industry groups. These studies have proven valuable in anticipating market, sector, and industry trends and lead RIS's portfolio managers to over- or underweight sectors in its client portfolios.

In explaining the importance of correctly identifying the proper sector, Jim Brady, senior vice president, stated:

> Anyone who doubts our big picture and sector analysis needs to just think back over the past 20 years of history and review some of the significant events and their impact on stock prices. In the early 1970s, we rolled into the decade with wage and price controls which regulated how much you pay your workers and how much you could charge your customers. In 1973 and 1979, we were faced with oil embargos. In between, we had tremendous bouts of wage and price inflation coupled with skyrocketing commodity prices in gold, silver, copper, corn, wheat, beef, coffee, sugar, and cocoa. In the 1980s, we were introduced to junk bond financing which created a form of financial Darwinism (weak companies were eaten by the strong). The bottom line of whether or not you made money depends on what you owned and when you owned it.

Three low-functional, obsolescent, consumer-goods stocks—Campbell Soup Company, Hershey Foods Corporation, and Kellogg Company—provide a perfect example of why sector/ industry selection is so important in determining investment portfolio performance (Exhibit 10–3). From 1974 to 1980, Kellogg Company's earnings grew at 16 percent annually, with dividend growth compounding at 14.3 percent per year. The return on Kellogg Company stock over that eight-year period was *zero!* Conversely, from 1981 to 1986, Kellogg Company provided a compounded rate of return of 566 percent although earnings slowed to 15.6 percent and dividend growth compounded at a lower 10.5 percent per year. Why the difference? The market rewarded those companies that produced commodities versus those which used commodities. With inflation running high from 1974 to 1980, these three commodity users suffered. When inflation and agricultural commodity prices began their downward spiral in 1981, these three stocks took off like rockets. Again, it is not only important what is owned but *when* it's owned.

As illustrated in Exhibits 10–3 and 10–4 (three oil-related stocks), stocks in the same sector or industry follow similar price patterns—when one is in favor, they all are in favor. As an extension of this fact, RIS believes an investor should purchase a basket of stocks representing the favored sector rather than trying to determine which stock within a sector is going to appreciate. Portfolio manager Deborah Grossman stated, "If we like the auto sector, we will purchase Ford, GM, and possibly Chrysler. Or if we like the airlines, we will allocate our client portfolio funds to United, Delta, and American Airlines."

Additionally, rather than concentrating on buy candidates, RIS allocates its resources and time to eliminating companies that do not belong in the basket due to quality (balance sheet) problems. Portfolio manager Salvatore Tartaglione added, "Any set of rules you use that pays attention to credit quality will invariably enhance portfolio performance and damper volatility. You don't have to baby-sit quality companies with sound financials. Our objective is to develop a basket of reasonable holdings representing our favored sector without balance sheet risks."

The role of Regent's research staff is to act as the translator between Safian's work and the investment strategy group and portfolio managers. Essentially, it filters through the mass of Safian's research and data to provide a three-part examination:

EXHIBIT 10–3
Consumer Sector (Foods)

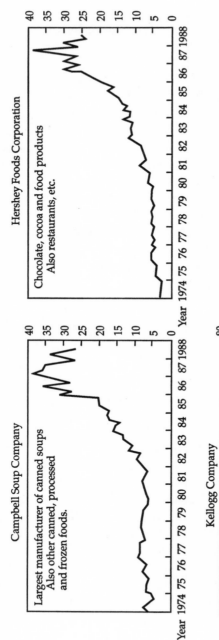

Campbell Soup Company

Largest manufacturer of canned soups
Also other canned, processed
and frozen foods.

Kellogg Company

Leading manufacturer of ready-to-eat cereals
and convenience food products

Period 1

Period 2

Year 1974 75 76 77 78 79 80 81 82 83 84 85 86 87 1988

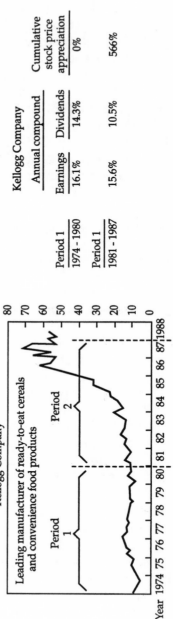

Hershey Foods Corporation

Chocolate, cocoa and food products
Also restaurants, etc.

Year 1974 75 76 77 78 79 80 81 82 83 84 85 86 87 1988

Kellogg Company

	Annual compound		Cumulative stock price appreciation
	Earnings	Dividends	
Period 1 1974 - 1980	16.1%	14.3%	0%
Period 1 1981 - 1987	15.6%	10.5%	566%

EXHIBIT 10–4
Energy Sector (Oil Producers)

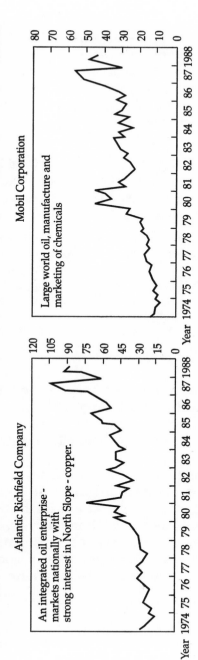

Atlantic Richfield Company

An integrated oil enterprise - markets nationally with strong interest in North Slope - copper.

Year 1974 75 76 77 78 79 80 81 82 83 84 85 86 87 1988

120 105 90 75 60 45 30 15 0

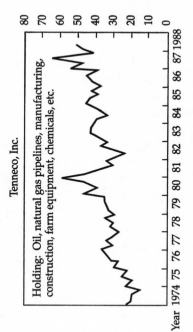

Mobil Corporation

Large world oil, manufacture and marketing of chemicals

Year 1974 75 76 77 78 79 80 81 82 83 84 85 86 87 1988

80 70 60 50 40 30 20 10 0

Tenneco, Inc.

Holding: Oil, natural gas pipelines, manufacturing, construction, farm equipment, chemicals, etc.

Year 1974 75 76 77 78 79 80 81 82 83 84 85 86 87 1988

80 70 60 50 40 30 20 10 0

1. Three-to-five-year, long-term themes. These are the non-quantifiable, three-to-five-year secular and economic trends impacting America. Examples include today's need for infrastructure rebuilding, revamping of our educational system, and improved waste treatment and retrieval systems.

2. Sector-relative earnings and valuations (one-to-two-year horizon). Looking out one to two years, which sectors look the most attractive from both an anticipated earnings and a valuation standpoint? Harold Stein explained,

> For example, you may identify that the auto sector earnings outlook is improving. Next we have to determine if and how much of this change has already been anticipated and is reflected in the market price. Currently [second quarter 1992], we are overweighted to the cyclical sector to reflect our anticipated economic activity improvement, but we will be quick to take over profits as the stock prices reflect this economic pickup. In other words, we don't want to overstay our welcome.

3. Earnings surprises and revisions. Although only used for short-term tactical decisions, earnings revisions and surprises are closely monitored to allow the research team to identify early trend changes. Stein continued, "Generally, positive surprises are replicated."

Also, Stein is careful to point out that he would never "bet his mortgage" on the short-term earnings indicator. It is just too unpredictable. Rather, he suggests investors focus on the first two indicators—the big picture and sector rotation analysis. He explained, "To be successful as an investor, you must trust your long-term economic theme analysis and buy a basket of stocks that represent your thinking." In reviewing RIS's long-term performance, Stein stated,

> Our most profitable positions came from decisions we made 6 to 18 months ago where we made early entries into sectors that were weak and unloved by the general investment world. We rarely attain instant gratification from our purchases. Although painful at times, it takes

time for our stocks to bear fruit. Additionally, having a large asset base to manage, making purchases on weakness mitigates our liquidity difficulties—we have no trouble buying good stocks when no one else wants them.

RIS adds value to these decisions through the examination and development of a proprietary database of unique relationships. The following are examples of indicators RIS considers during different market environments to help it in determining sector weightings:

1. Relative yields of RIS averages versus Treasury securities.
2. Relative earnings and price ratios for RIS's sector averages.
3. RIS growth stock universe relative earnings.
4. Historical price to earnings ratios.
5. Six-month and annual price momentum rates.

For the overall market, RIS looks at some key indicators, such as:

1. Monetary indicators—money supply/GNP.
2. Sentiment data—investors' intelligence.
3. Liquidity measures.
4. Savings/debt—consumer, corporate.
5. Corporate earnings and cash flow multiples.

RIS attempts to get out in front into sectors before it becomes fashionable to be investing in that asset class. In other words, it tries to stay ahead of the public wave. As John Templeton has regularly said, "If you invest the same way everyone else does, you'll have everyone else's results."

Since RIS's overall goals are consistent performance coupled with low volatility, it prefers not to make big bets in one sector or another, even when its model and economic sector work indicate that these sectors represent an excellent value and opportunity. By overweighting its favorite sector and underweighting the least attractive areas, RIS exposes its clients to potential capital appreciation without betting the farm, as a pure value manager may do.

EXHIBIT 10–5
Yield Curve (January 31, 1992)

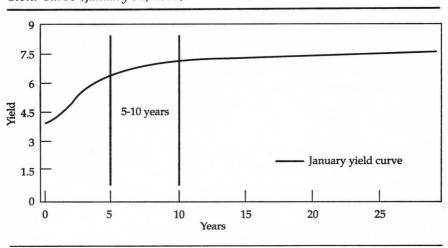

III.   FIXED-INCOME STRATEGY—BALANCING RISK WITH HIGH CURRENT INCOME

As a balanced manager, RIS pursues a similar approach and philosophy in selecting bonds. It stresses that bonds must be actively managed, as they are not the safe harbor that many investors believe them to be. RIS prefers U.S. Treasury and agency bonds and purchases only those corporate bonds rated A or better. In other words, quality is emphasized.

RIS is an intermediate-duration bond manager with an emphasis on reduction of volatility. Its intermediate (5–10 years) average life approach has produced rates of return associated with longer-maturity bonds without their dramatic price risk and volatility. The portfolio managers use a tactic called "investing at the shoulder of the yield curve." In Exhibit 10–5, the yield curve line resembles an arm, then begins to plateau, forming what looks like a shoulder.

Specifically, RIS invests in maturities ranging from the top of the arm/beginning of the shoulder to the neck (which, in this example, is between 5 and 10 years). By staying in this tight maturity

EXHIBIT 10–6
The Business Cycle and the Effect on the Bond Market

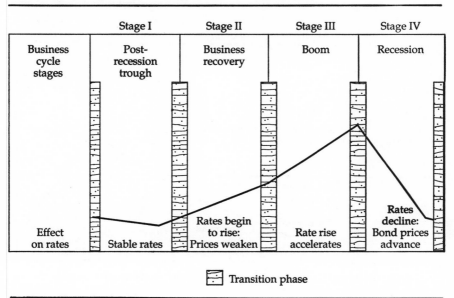

	Stage I	Stage II	Stage III	Stage IV
Business cycle stages	Post-recession trough	Business recovery	Boom	Recession
Effect on rates	Stable rates	Rates begin to rise: Prices weaken	Rate rise accelerates	Rates decline: Bond prices advance

 Transition phase

range, RIS is able to obtain 90 percent of the yield of a 30-year bond with half the volatility and risk of the longer maturities.

Furthermore, RIS attempts to add value by achieving these strategic objectives:

1. Forecasting secular changes in interest rates.
2. Making maturity and duration judgments to maximize returns based on interest-rate forecasts.
3. Weighting sectors (Treasury, agency, corporate) on the basis of proprietary valuation methods supported by external research sources. Maturity, duration of portfolios, and sector weightings are derived from expectations for interest rates and risk/reward analysis among market sectors. Portfolios are actively managed and monitored continually, with portfolio characteristics (maturity, duration, and sector composition) adapted to changing rate environments. This process is outlined in Exhibits 10–6 and 10–7. For example, if the economy is in Stage II,

EXHIBIT 10–7
Fixed Income (Investment Discipline)

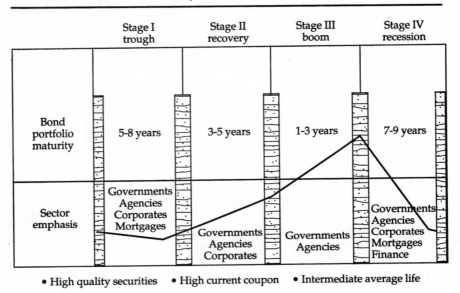

	Stage I trough	Stage II recovery	Stage III boom	Stage IV recession
Bond portfolio maturity	5-8 years	3-5 years	1-3 years	7-9 years
Sector emphasis	Governments Agencies Corporates Mortgages	Governments Agencies Corporates	Governments Agencies	Governments Agencies Corporates Mortgages Finance

• High quality securities   • High current coupon   • Intermediate average life

recovery, and interest rates are beginning to rise, then three- to five-year government agencies and corporates will be emphasized in client portfolios.

IV.   PUTTING IT ALL TOGETHER— CONSTRUCTING A CLIENT PORTFOLIO

The investment process, from Safian's analytical work to actual portfolio construction, is charted in Exhibit 10–8. First, investment ideas originate from a thorough review and study of pertinent economic, political, and fundamental factors that have proven valuable in anticipating market, sector, and industry group trends. This information is filtered through the director of equity research and fixed income, who in turn condenses and organizes the information for the investment strategy group.

The investment strategy committee has direct responsibility for

EXHIBIT 10–8
*The Investment Process: **Putting It All Together** (Constructing the Client Portfolio)*

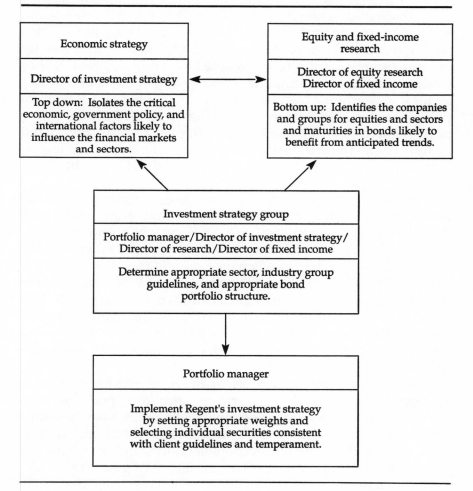

all investment-related policies and guidelines. The managing directors have formal meetings on a monthly basis where strategic, long-term plans are reviewed and modified. Weekly meetings, including members of the research, marketing, trading, and administrative departments, are held to discuss investment strategy, new business, and operational concerns. As with any good investment advisory house, there is an informal, free-flowing atmosphere within RIS where ideas are exchanged throughout the day.

As discussed earlier in the strategy section, RIS uses sector rotation as its principal approach to equity investing. Rather than relying on a top-down or market timing approach, or a bottom-up or stock picking approach, it has opted for a middle ground, with concentration on analyzing the economy and equity markets on a sectoral and group basis. RIS believes that consistent long-term performance is best obtained by making diversified commitments to broad sectors of the market (growth over cyclical stocks) and by uncovering those industry groups that will benefit from important changes in the economic, political, and demographic landscapes.

Overall asset allocation decisions are determined by the director of investment strategy and the investment strategy group in accordance with its continuous evaluation of current economic conditions. Each portfolio manager takes into consideration specific client goals and guidelines when incorporating asset allocation per account. RIS will gladly assist the client in forming an investment policy, and investment guidelines can then be modified to best address these needs. Currently (June 1992), RIS is investing balanced portfolios by allocating 55 percent in equities, 35 percent in fixed income, and 10 percent in cash equivalents. (This asset allocation changes frequently.)

Portfolio managers working independently with the director of research carefully review investment selections, pertinent supporting analysis, and suggested buying strategies. Managers then confer to make selections from among large capitalized companies. They will incorporate recommendations into portfolios for which they are responsible, within each client's guidelines.

Portfolio managers, trading, and research work together to determine entry weightings. Equity positions usually take the form of a percentage of equity holdings. For example, companies in the paper industry may represent 7 percent of the equity holdings. Various weightings in companies such as Weyerhauser 2 percent, International Paper 1.5 percent, Union Camp 1.5 percent, and so on, would comprise this total.

The specific buy and sell disciplines are as follows:

Buy disciplines

1. Determine which sectors and industry groups will be the principal beneficiaries of economic, political, and technical factors.
2. Director of research and the investment strategy committee identify companies within validated sectors and industry groups; fundamental and technical research is completed on the appropriate companies.
3. Individual portfolio managers select individual issues best suited to client needs.
4. Portfolio positions in individual stocks run 1 to 4 percent of total equity holdings. (Weightings depend on the size of industry group and sectors.)
5. Portfolio managers determine entry ranges and coordinate purchases with the equity trader.

Sell disciplines

1. When a holding reaches its projected value.
2. When an event changes the anticipated value of an individual holding.
3. When the director of investment strategy and the investment strategy committee implement a reduction in an industry or sector weighting, the least desirable holding is eliminated.
4. When an opportunity in a sector or industry occurs, the least desirable holding is swapped.
5. When the director of investment strategy and the investment strategy committee implement a reduction in equity investment levels, the securities are sold to reduce exposure.

Each portfolio is continually reviewed by its portfolio manager, assistant, and assigned backup. The principal responsibility of the manager is to ensure that portfolios are structured consistently with the goals, objectives, and guidelines of the client and the investment framework established by the director of investment strategy and investment strategy committee.

EXHIBIT 10–9
Risk/Reward Analysis—Balanced (10-Year Quarterly Returns through
December 31, 1991)

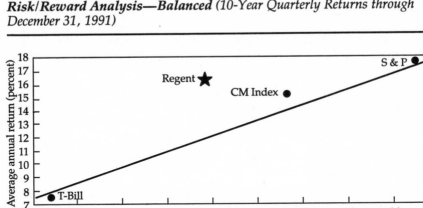

	Ten year composite return	Standard deviation
Regent	16.1	7.4
CM Index	15.5	11.4
S & P	17.6	16.8

Every portfolio's performance is reviewed and compared weekly to other client portfolios managed by the same person and those of other managers. Members of the management committee meet to monitor adherence to policy and performance.

V. SUMMARY—CONSISTENCY AND LOW VOLATILITY

What is impressive about RIS's performance is not only the demonstrated average annual rates of return, but the way they were accomplished. As seen in Exhibit 10–9, in balanced portfolios, RIS outperformed the capital markets' balanced index (stocks, bonds, cash) and did it with about 60 percent of the capital markets' risk or

EXHIBIT 10–10
Fixed-Income Returns (1977–1991)

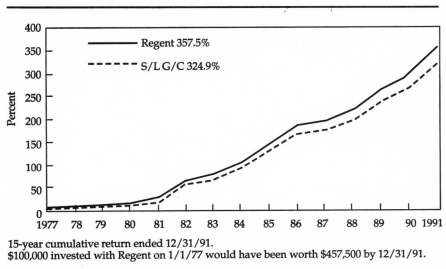

15-year cumulative return ended 12/31/91.
$100,000 invested with Regent on 1/1/77 would have been worth $457,500 by 12/31/91.

volatility. Also, over the 10-year period ending December 31, 1991, RIS's annual returns were within 1.5 percent per year of the S&P 500, yet its average portfolio consisted of a 52 percent bond exposure with the remaining funds split between stocks and cash. In other words, RIS was able to generate S&P-like returns while holding a majority of client assets in safer, less volatile, short- to intermediate-term, high-quality bonds.

RIS's style is appropriate for investors seeking the most conservative, balanced approach. While it will never hit any home runs, RIS's consistency is hard to dispute. Like a strong, steady center on a basketball team, RIS may not flash up big numbers, but it is the backbone of the team and can be counted on for its consistent play. As shown in Exhibits 10–10, 10–11, and 10–12, for the past 10 years, RIS has outperformed the indices in all three markets—fixed-income, balanced, and equity indices.

When does this portfolio approach not work as effectively? During isolated time periods, the macroeconomic view may be less

EXHIBIT 10–11
Balanced Fund Returns (1982–1991)

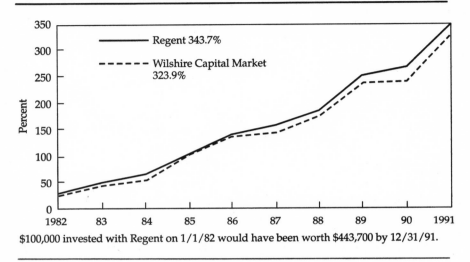

$100,000 invested with Regent on 1/1/82 would have been worth $443,700 by 12/31/91.

valuable than other times. For example, when monetary and/or tax policy provides for speculative investing instead of economically based investing, as was evident during the takeover period of the 1980s, then RIS's style will most likely lag the market leaders. During these aberrations, RIS's approach is to monitor the underlying economic trends, thereby resulting in a conservative, less speculative portfolio construction.

RIS, with Safian's research leadership, prides itself on its proprietary database and is continually searching for new enhancements. For example, the composite forecasting index (CFI) created in 1984 allows the firm to zero in on the economy and its segments. According to RIS, the CFI is not only more focused than the government's statistical models, but it is also more accurate. Recently, RIS has uncovered several helpful indicators of economic activity. As a measure of plant and equipment expenditures, it examines nondefense capital goods, less aircraft and parts (because aircraft orders can have such a dramatic impact overshadowing the whole series). For an indication of the consumer's

EXHIBIT 10–12
Equity Returns (1977–1991)

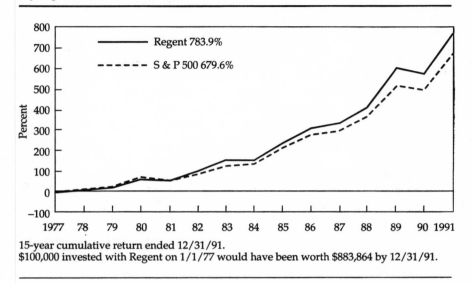

15-year cumulative return ended 12/31/91.
$100,000 invested with Regent on 1/1/77 would have been worth $883,864 by 12/31/91.

ability to stimulate the economy, retail sales, less automobile and gasoline sales, are monitored.

Trying to forecast the direction of the economy and its sectors is a dangerous occupation. More than a few investment advisers have shortened their investment careers by making incorrect bets on the direction of the fickle U.S. economy. Very few advisers have demonstrated an ability to perform such a feat on a consistent basis. RIS is one manager that has demonstrated clairvoyance and believes it can continue to anticipate the trends.

One of the key lessons demonstrated by Safian and RIS is that one does not have to be a crackerjack stock picker to succeed in the market. Instead, if you have the ability, time, inclination, and resources to approach and analyze where the economy stands and how the various industries and sectors fit into this scenario, the necessary framework is built for a sector-driven portfolio. The second important lesson passed on by RIS is that, rather than attempting to pick the best specific stock, such as Merck & Co.,

Glaxo Holdings PLC, Bristol-Myers Squibb, Syntex Corp., Schering-Plough Corp., Eli Lilly & Co., or Upjohn Co. (which RIS views as being almost impossible), build a drug sector basket of stocks.

Although RIS and Shields Asset Management manage over $7 billion, they do it with a very small staff. Focusing on economic facts and sector analysis does not require layer upon layer of individual stock analysts. One of the strengths of the two firms and a contribution to their overall effectiveness is the lack of a large bureaucratic organization in which to make decisions. The smallness of RIS and Safian's group promotes an informal decision-making style. Large staffs would get in the way of these constant informal conversations, thereby creating obstacles to communication and reducing overall effectiveness.

Its top-down, sector-rotation style is consistently applied and has proven effective throughout varying market cycles. RIS has implemented this style since its founding and feels that the style will continue to allow it to adjust to future economic cycles. RIS has never deviated from and does not anticipate altering its style.

For most investors, gauging, evaluating, and interpreting economic, political, and social trends is not an easy task. In fact, in most cases, it is a mistake to even try! Ken Safian and the investment professionals at RIS bring to mind a quote made by Ken Fisher of Fisher Investments. When discussing investors' analytical investment abilities, he stated, "It's OK to spend a lot of time thinking—as long as you're a good thinker. Otherwise, thinking is going to get you in a lot of trouble." Although most investor egos will not admit it, they would be better off letting the professionals like Regent Investment Services handle the economic forecasting.

Chapter Eleven

Rittenhouse Financial Services
The Pure Blue-Chip Investment Adviser

The old real estate adage of only buying property in the best neighborhood aptly describes Rittenhouse Financial Services' (RFS) stock and bond portfolio philosophy. Its portfolio managers do not seek out bargains or small companies with spectacular growth potential characteristics. Rather, they focus strictly and narrowly on large, well-capitalized household names that have demonstrated earnings and/or dividend growth year after year.

In fact, an RFS client portfolio reads like the *who's who* of leading American business. AT&T, Johnson & Johnson, The Coca-Cola Company, Merck, General Electric Co., and Wal-Mart Stores, Inc. are just a few of the 25 to 35 industry leaders making up RFS's core blue-chip portfolio.

Rittenhouse espouses a long-term, bullish outlook and therefore does not react to short-term market gyrations or investor whims; nor does it try to outguess the market with market timing tactics. RFS portfolio managers do not feel that interpretation of investor psychology has much place in portfolio management except for the ultra-aggressive account.

As James S. Morgan, vice president and chief investment officer-equities stated, "Trying to guess the market direction over any short-term period is a fool's game."

Richard D. Hughes, executive vice president of Rittenhouse Capital Management, a wholly owned subsidiary, added, "Although we do make macroeconomic forecasts, these projections do not interfere with our ability to manage quality blue-chip stocks and bonds. Why should we venture to determine the direction of the economy when our nation's top economists cannot even give us an absolute answer?"

George W. Connell, founder and president of RFS, confirmed this attitude:

> No one has ever called more than four or five market turns in a row. In the past 30 years, there have been eight major upward moves. Had you missed one of these bull market moves, your long-term rate of return would have been significantly less than the S&P 500's long-term average. I believe investors make a big mistake by keeping 50 percent of their investable funds in cash because they believe the market is heading south. History has shown us that the market is more likely to go up, and then the investor is caught holding an empty bag. This creates additional anxiety because now the investor feels like he/she has missed the boat. Now the decision to get into the market is even more difficult. Is it too late, or should he/she pay up for stocks?

I. HISTORY OF RFS

George Connell first developed an interest in the stock market at age 11. His grandfather had been a governor of the stock exchange. After graduating from Wharton and working as a lower-level analyst at J. P. Morgan & Company, he joined Drexel & Company as an investment adviser where he was appointed corporate first vice president. For 20 years, Connell adeptly handled client portfolios, which included a position as the vice chairman for the top-ranked Burnham Fund and chairman of the Drexel Lambert investment adviser's portfolio review committee.

In the late 1970s, Connell felt like a fish out of water at Drexel. Not only was the firm dominated by Milken's record-setting, revenue-generating activities, but the firm's stock selection and portfolio management strategies were inconsistent with his philosophy. While Drexel believed in buying cyclical stocks and then actively trading the portfolio, Connell not only felt that noncyclical companies with consistent earnings and dividend growth were better candidates, but also believed that quality stocks should be held until their earnings and dividend growth matured.

He remembered "feeling like an outsider. Everything I espoused was alien to the Drexel culture. In addition, the management fees from our investment management services accounted for less than 1/10 of 1 percent of the firm's total revenues. Clearly, investment management services and my investment philosophy were not top priorities within the firm."

In 1979, Connell founded RFS. Located in Radnor, Pennsylvania, the firm serves a diversified list of clients, including corporate and employee benefit plans, charitable institutions, endowment funds, a mutual fund whose portfolio is confined to tax-free securities, private trusts, and accounts of wealthy individuals. With total assets of the combined corporations currently exceeding $5.3 billion, RFS offers a full range of investment management capabilities for equity, short-term, fixed-income, and tax-exempt funds on a discretionary or consultative basis.

Within RFS, three subsidiary organizations have been developed to further meet client needs—Rittenhouse Trust Company, Rittenhouse Capital Management, and Rittenhouse Financial Securities, Inc. The Rittenhouse Trust Company allows individuals to enhance their portfolio management with the continuity, protection, and planning benefits afforded by professional estate and trust arrangements. As a member of the Federal Reserve Bank of Philadelphia, the trust company also provides deposit and loan facilities for their clients as a value-added product. Rittenhouse Capital Management, Inc. manages some $3.5 billion of wrap accounts through its staff of 72, while devoting considerable energies to servicing brokerage clients. Rittenhouse Financial Securities, Inc., member of the National Association of Securities Dealers, is used for transactions only in smaller accounts which have not been introduced by a broker.

II. PHILOSOPHY—BLUE-CHIP SERVICE AND INVESTMENTS

A major premise of RFS's investment philosophy is that each client deserves a personalized and highly individualized approach to fulfill specific investment needs and objectives. The RFS portfolio managers spend tremendous amounts of time not only servicing their broker relationships but "holding the hands" of clients. Once a client's objectives have been fully clarified and identified, the RFS portfolio managers develop a portfolio of securities seeking premium investment returns while assuming a minimum of market risk. They believe that the preservation of capital under their management is a primary concern, but under extreme conditions, cash management becomes an important alternative. Preferably, they are fully invested at all times, whether it is an equity or a balanced account.

Beginning with a staff of only three, Connell has been successful in attracting managers who completely embrace this blue-chip style. RFS does not formally employ a marketing staff; rather, all account solicitation is left in the hands of its portfolio managers, investment management consultants, and brokerage houses. Believing that its prospective clients prefer to meet face-to-face with the individuals responsible for managing their funds, RFS investment managers spend a great deal of time meeting with clients. Each account has two portfolio managers so that under all conditions coverage can be provided. Currently, 78 people are members of the corporation, of which 27 are investment professionals.

The philosophy and strategies to which the RFS portfolio managers adhere have been employed by George Connell throughout his investment career. While attending the Wharton undergraduate School of Business, he completed a term paper testing the validity of "dollar cost averaging" (periodic investment of a set amount of funds) as a long-term investment strategy. He summarized his findings with these comments:

> I found dollar cost averaging to be a successful overall strategy as long as one concentrated his/her stock purchases to companies that demonstrated consistent earnings and dividend growth. In other words, it was the earnings and dividend growth that led to the positive results, not the dollar cost averaging. Dollar cost averaging can be disastrous if you fail to purchase stocks that are continually increasing in value. The message stuck with me and provided the framework from which I have managed for the past 30 years.

Compared to other equity and balanced managers, if RFS portfolio managers err, it has usually been on the side of conservatism. But this approach has helped its clients' overall, longer-term, total return performance. They have not been seduced by "fad" stocks, which if purchased in a timely manner may provide terrific returns, but are sure to disappoint if not exited before the fad runs its course.

III.   STRATEGY—SEPARATING THE WHEAT FROM THE CHAFF

RFS attempts to detect structural shifts in the economy which may cause major realignments in the equity and bond markets. Portfolio manager Deborah Manning stated,

> Structural shifts in the economy are frequently gradual, rarely obvious. In the volatile markets of recent years, it has become essential to identify the point at which gradual change is accelerating to produce a different economic environment. The changed environment can be depended on to revise the list of highly profitable industries—and of rewarding investment options.

A.   Fixed Income

As a starting point, a client's assets are efficiently allocated between debt and equity securities. Primarily, the 35 percent of assets invested in fixed income are to provide income, emphasizing higher-quality issues (A or better) with the investment spread over maturities up to 10 years (five-year average life).

Connell and his staff recognize the importance of fixed income in reducing portfolio risk and dampening volatility in balanced accounts as well as being a source of income. At the helm of RFS bond decision strategy is Leonard H. McCandless, vice president and chief investment officer-fixed income. In describing his overall fixed-income strategy, McCandless states,

> We have tended to avoid long-term issues, believing that the incremental return did not justify the risk. Being very much aware of the spreads that might exist between the government and corporate sectors at opportune times, the fixed-income positions of clients' portfolios are actively managed in an attempt to capitalize on opportunities

EXHIBIT 11-1
The Rittenhouse Fixed-Income Decision Process

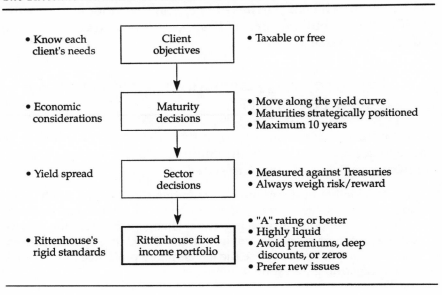

• Know each client's needs	**Client objectives**	• Taxable or free
• Economic considerations	**Maturity decisions**	• Move along the yield curve • Maturities strategically positioned • Maximum 10 years
• Yield spread	**Sector decisions**	• Measured against Treasuries • Always weigh risk/reward
• Rittenhouse's rigid standards	**Rittenhouse fixed income portfolio**	• "A" rating or better • Highly liquid • Avoid premiums, deep discounts, or zeros • Prefer new issues

available during interest rate cycles. Municipal bonds are held in the accounts of substantial individual investors.

He keeps a constant lookout for possible rating downgrades and alerts the RFS portfolio managers so that portfolio modifications can be initiated before a severe decline. The RFS fixed-income decision process is outlined in Exhibit 11–1.

B. Stock Selection

Clients' assets are spread between 25 to 35 core stock holdings from a potential buy candidate list of 100 securities. It is the selection process and management of these core holdings that defines and distinguishes RFS from other blue-chip money managers. Its track record of double-digit rates of return coupled with unusually low volatility is a direct result of the unwaivering adherence to an investment criteria. This process is graphically depicted in Exhibit 11–2.

EXHIBIT 11–2
The Rittenhouse Equity Investment Process (A Top-Down Approach Without Market Timing)

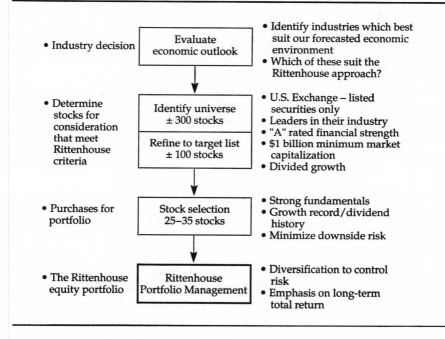

• Industry decision	Evaluate economic outlook	• Identify industries which best suit our forecasted economic environment • Which of these suit the Rittenhouse approach?
• Determine stocks for consideration that meet Rittenhouse criteria	Identify universe ± 300 stocks Refine to target list ± 100 stocks	• U.S. Exchange – listed securities only • Leaders in their industry • "A" rated financial strength • $1 billion minimum market capitalization • Divided growth
• Purchases for portfolio	Stock selection 25–35 stocks	• Strong fundamentals • Growth record/dividend history • Minimize downside risk
• The Rittenhouse equity portfolio	Rittenhouse Portfolio Management	• Diversification to control risk • Emphasis on long-term total return

In all of its investments, the word *quality* cannot be overemphasized, with investments never made in either stocks or bonds rated below A by the rating services unless otherwise directed in writing by the client. RFS buys what it considers to be franchise stocks—companies with dominant market share. Its portfolio managers attempt to take advantage of the dichotomy or pricing inefficiencies that exist among their franchise candidates. Basically, RFS feels it gains an advantage over competitors in correctly identifying growth patterns. As stated earlier, growth of earnings and especially of dividends is a prerequisite of the company's basic strategy. And with quality of paramount importance, many of the industrial classifications of the S&P 500 are eliminated entirely. Moreover, since speculative situations are never included on the approved list of stocks from which they operate, this list has a volatility rating in line with the market (overall beta 1.04) and a low debt-to-capital ratio amounting to only, on average, 27 percent.

With portfolios made up of stocks of this nature, they are sure to underperform for short periods in surging bull, upside moves, but holdings fare far better in periods of weakness with higher-than-average earnings and constantly expanding yields. The RFS track record is superior. The firm believes this performance has been achieved by the purchase of dominant companies which are able to prosper in both good and bad economic times. While superior yields would be nice, the growth of dividends seems of greater importance in gauging ultimate value. Over the years, the pursuit of this strategy has fared well under a variety of economic conditions. (See Exhibit 11–3.)

C.   *Putting It All Together*

Once the blue-chip stocks have been identified, RFS goes one step further—it groups its 100 buy list candidates into three distinct profiles: (1) long-term growth; (2) moderate growth; and (3) cyclical growth. This method arose from the belief that one of the most important aspects of portfolio management is systematic allocation of funds to specific types of investments, depending on the objectives of various accounts and the prevailing economic and investment environment.

Typically, with most investment advisers, the allocation of investment funds within an account is based on random selection, dictated by what looks good at the moment, paying little or no attention to how a particular selection fits into the range of investments appropriate for the account's purposes. The result, most often, is a clustering of holdings in the great middle ground of quality and value, producing only average long-term growth.

When a guideline is used in the deployment of funds, most frequently it is the traditional method of diversification by industry. Yet, because of the range of performance and quality available within an industry, allocating a percentage of funds to an industry has little meaning in itself and frequently leads to an inaccurate description of a portfolio's position in relation to its objectives or the expected environment.

EXHIBIT 11–3
The Rittenhouse Equity Portfolio: The Proof Statement

Standards	Produce Results
• Companies must be "A" rated or better	• Average rating in portfolios is A+
• Companies must have a minimum market capitalization of $1 billion	• Average market capitalization is $14 billion
• Companies must lead their industries	• Franchise companies dominate portfolios
• Invest for total return: Capital appreciation plus dividend income	• Annualized compound return past ten years exceeds 20 percent*
• Place emphasis on above-average annual dividend growth	• Stocks have consistently increased their dividends —Triple the inflation rate —Double the S&P 500
• Control risk via diversified portfolios	• Typically 25–35 stocks in 18–23 industries —Leading companies provide global diversification —Average portfolio beta is 1.00

* See performance data for basis of computations.

In search of a better system, RFS first established its criteria: What precisely does a given security bring to the portfolio? What requirements does it meet? How does it fit into the expected structure of economic growth? The firm then developed a series of portfolio profiles to show more accurately the characteristics of various types of stocks as they relate to portfolio strategy. These profiles are classifications of companies having a high degree of similarity in such characteristics as financial and managerial quality, industry position, long-term outlook, general level of valuation relative to the stock market, sensitivity to cyclical fluctuations, type of risk, and potential reward. Each profile displays a combination of qualities unique to that group. These profiles help determine which groups are most appropriate for an account's objectives and also help make the client aware of the shortcomings of particular groups. These groups present a wide range of alternatives in value, risk, income production, and potential capital appreciation. They also present a logical way to allocate funds based on the needs and objectives of the account.

Each of the three profiles is outlined in the following section with the risks and possible rewards, as well as the common characteristics.

1. Long-term rapid growth. This group is limited to companies that are experiencing sales and earnings gains of 10 percent or better annually. To qualify, a company must be a leading factor in its industry; it must be soundly financed; and the product line must be either broad or well-protected from competitors by patents or by an accumulation of skills not readily duplicated. While this may appear redundant in light of the preceding requirements, management must give evidence of unusual capability. Examples include Merck & Co., The Coca-Cola Company, Johnson & Johnson, Bristol-Myers Co., Wal-Mart Stores, Inc., General Mills, Inc., and Procter & Gamble.

As a group, these companies usually sell at a large premium over the general market level. In periods of sharp market weakness, these stocks can decline as much as 50 percent from a preceding high for no reason except an end to premium pricing.

On the other hand, successful investments in this group over the years have exceeded any popular measure of market performance by a wide margin. For accounts seeking maximum, long-term performance, capable of foregoing current income, and financially and emotionally able to ride through some wide price fluctuations, representation in this group is appropriate. In assessing the group, RFS feels it represents maximum short-term price risk, minimum quality risk, and maximum long-term reward potential.

2. Moderate growth. This profile group is restricted to high-quality companies that appear to have a well-assured ability to increase sales and earnings by about 6 to 10 percent annually. By definition, the group's profits generally must be relatively impervious to changes in the level of economic activity. Examples include the telephone companies, E. I. du Pont de Nemours & Company, and Dun & Bradstreet. The stocks in this group tend to sell at some premium over the general market level. Generally, they are not subject to as wide price swings as either the rapid growth or the cyclical growth stocks. As long-term holdings, they should offer earnings growth in excess of the general economy. If RFS assumes a constant valuation of earnings, this group should offer price appreciation potential of 100 percent every 6 to 10 years. This group is particularly attractive during periods of economic plateauing or downturn. If the account is sufficiently flexible, these stocks can be used as replacements for the cyclical growth issues on an intermediate basis.

3. **Cyclical growth.** For its purposes, RFS considers stocks in this group to be in industries that experience peak-to-peak or trough-to-trough growth exceeding that of the economy. This group is confined to top-quality companies, both financially and by management capability. Examples include Union Pacific Corporation, Dover Corporation, and ITT Corporation.

Bought near a cyclical bottom of activity in their industry, these stocks represent excellent quality and value. Held over any subsequent economic recovery, they can provide well-above-average price performance. Such investments are a valid means of minimizing price and quality risk while offering the possibility of above-average price appreciation during the period of cyclical expansion. When this group is used for such a purpose, a timing risk is injected at both ends of the program. They can be bought too soon and turn in no performance for a period of time, or they can be sold too soon or too late in the cycle. If this profile group is held as a long-term investment, it is done with the realization that the long-term growth will be about the same as that of the economy.

Unless the client specifies otherwise, RFS portfolio managers prefer to place 70 to 80 percent of equity allocations in the rapid-growth section, 10 to 20 percent in the moderate-growth area, and no more than 10 percent in the cyclical-growth category. If a client had no income requirements and was willing to accept wide fluctuations in portfolio value, then emphasis in long-term rapid-growth stocks would be appropriate. In discussing its client base, Deborah Manning said,

Most clients do not have the tolerance or psychological makeup to handle higher portfolio volatility; therefore, a balanced portfolio such as 65 percent stocks, 35 percent medium-term bonds, with the equity portion split between rapid and moderate growth, makes the most sense. Cyclical growth will only be emphasized during a plateau or recession. We try to give our clients a good balance of present value, income, long-term growth, capital appreciation, and insulation from cyclical risk.

A meeting of the entire staff is held weekly, and the outlook for the economy and the equity and fixed-income market is reviewed. This is followed by a series of account reviews, so that in the course of a year all portfolios are examined several times. All of the portfolio managers are members of, and participate in, the actions of the stock selection committee designating the specific stocks that should be represented in most of the accounts under management. Dollar diversification among the industrial groups included is the responsibility of the manager in accordance with each client's needs and objectives within prescribed industry weightings. However, any divergence in the investment style and philosophy must have the approval of this group.

RFS is careful to stay away from stocks selling at premium multiples where a negative earnings surprise will decimate the stock. Jim Morgan passed along a simple rule when buying stocks:

Analysts' projected earnings growth must have a reasonable relationship to the price/earnings ratio. For example, a stock we sold was Waste Management. Although we liked the long-term prospects of the company, the projected earnings were expected to increase by about 20 percent, and the P/E ratio stood at 28—too rich for our blood. One must make sure not to pay too much for a particular company—even if it dominates its industry.

RFS's experience has shown that in a carefully selected portfolio of 25 to 35 core stocks, several will exceed the firm's expectations and several will disappoint the firm. The others will continue to clip along at a 10 to 20 percent annual growth rate. In addition, RFS believes each client should have some energy exposure as an inflation hedge; also, these stocks offer excellent value. Their long-

EXHIBIT 11-4
The RAP Chart (Report of Accumulative Performance)

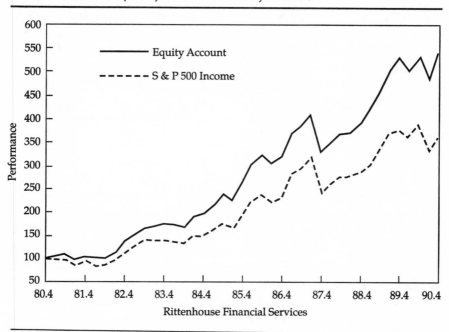

Source: RS&A Consulting, Inc.

term favorites include The Royal Dutch/Shell Group, Mobil Oil Corp., and Exxon Corporation.

While the individual managers may make portfolio changes as they see fit, the decision to make broad sales through the removal of an individual stock from the approved list requires action by the entire stock selection committee. If one of the primary stocks falls behind the market performance of others in its industry classification, its revenues and earnings vary materially, or its growth rate is maturing/moderating, it is carefully scrutinized and placed on a short-term watch list. If the reason can be determined and is viewed as a lingering situation, the stock is removed. If questions are answered favorably, the stock will be retained in the list, and, indeed, even averaging down is recommended. A particular issue will be sold if the price gain is outpacing the earnings and dividend growth.

A fully invested approach will never outperform the market timer who is able to move to 100 percent cash just before a major market downturn. But, on a relative basis, RFS has performed admirably. For example, in 1990, when the market sold off 20 percent due to the Iraqi invasion of Kuwait, the average RFS portfolio was only off 7 percent. Rittenhouse has the standards; do they produce the results? Exhibit 11–4 summarizes its effectiveness.

IV. SUMMARY

Since 1979, RFS's balanced accounts have averaged close to 17 percent, with 35 percent less than a fully invested position in equities. In pure equity accounts, RFS portfolios have averaged close to 20 percent, with 7 percent less risk than the overall stock market. For whom would Rittenhouse's style be appropriate? Investors desiring blue-chip, franchise companies that dominate their particular industry groups will be especially attracted to RFS.

Looking out to the next decade, RFS sees the Dow at 4000 to 5000 before the year 2000. George Connell commented,

> RFS will continue to focus on high-quality, large capitalization, excellent financial strength, consistent earnings, and/or dividend growth type of companies. We will not be tempted to modify our style—even if we lag the overall markets. We have been able to avoid disasters by sticking to our guns. We are confident that our disciplined style will continue to meet our client expectations.

Staying on the train with Rittenhouse has richly rewarded its clients.

The Rittenhouse portfolio management team has given many public seminars on money management over the last several years. According to Richard Hughes, one of the themes that has always been presented is "discipline and consistency." The Rittenhouse organization believes that a discipline has to be applied day in and day out in order to achieve superior, consistent results.

In the seminars, Hughes, like Roger Engemann, likes to use the train analogy, leaving the audiences with:

The stock market is like a northbound train. Its starting point is Miami, Florida, and the final destination is Portland, Maine. The train is in Savanah, Georgia, now. It may go back to Jacksonville, Florida, to pick up more passengers, but it may not. Unfortunately, some passengers may get off the train. However, if your destination is Portland, get on board the train today and stay on board because it is definitely going to arrive at its destination.

Chapter Twelve

Systematic Financial Management, Inc.
Return of the Accounting Nerds

"Go where the money is."

Willie Sutton, bank robber

Efficient market theoreticians may tell you that it is impossible to obtain higher-than-market returns without investing in securities with risks that exceed the market's. Systematic will resist settling for the easy response to this proposition: just look at Systematic's performance results. That response would be illustrative, yet overly simple and incomplete. In addition, disciples of the efficient market theory would respond that, statistically, a few managers will always outperform the market (i.e., get lucky). The more earnest response is that Systematic's clients benefit from information and analyses not generally available to other investors.

No, Systematic's investments do not involve insider trading or other illicit activities! For more than 10 years, Kenneth S. Hackel, Systematic's founder and president, has used publicly available information regarding companies' cash flows to develop a proprietary methodology for evaluating intrinsic value. That methodology determines what Systematic calls *free cash flow*—the maximum amount of cash a company can pay out in dividends or reinvest in the company. As a bottom up stock picker, Systemic goes to where the free cash flow is.

Systematic uses cash flow information in a way that no other investment adviser has.[1] A basic assumption of the efficient mar-

---

[1] See Kenneth S. Hackel and Joshua Livnat, *Cash Flow and Security Analysis* (Homewood, Ill.: Business One Irwin, 1992).

EXHIBIT 12–1
Equity Moderately Conservative Managers Risk/Return Analysis from 1981 through 1991

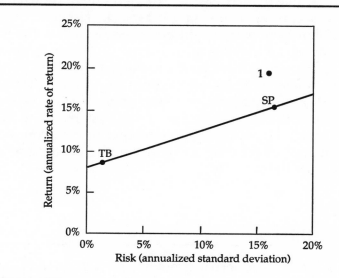

Prudential Securities
Investment manager scatterchart information for equity moderately conservative managers (from 1981 through 1991)

Key	Manager	Return	Risk (S.D.)	Sharpe
1	Systematic	19.48%	16.09%	0.68
SP	S&P 500	15.27	16.59	0.40
TB	T-Bills	8.56	1.33	0.00

ket theory is that all investors benefit from the same information. That assumption is violated when investors choose to disregard what may be the most valuable information available to them— cash flow—and instead give inappropriate weight to reported earnings, which often distort a company's true operating results.

Exhibit 12–1 reflects the investment performance and risk of the investment portfolios managed by Systematic, as monitored by Global Perspectives, Inc., an independent consulting firm.

The efficient portfolio theory would require that all portfolios fall on the line which intersects the risk and reward level of U.S.

Treasury bills, which are risk-free investments, and of the market portfolio reflected by the S&P 500 index. In other words, an investor should be able to increase the expected rate of return only by purchasing securities involving greater risk. However, Systematic's portfolios have been significantly less risky than the market and have achieved average annual returns which theoretically should be reserved for those who are willing to invest in portfolios so risky that they would fall off the right edge of this diagram.

Exhibit 12–2 illustrates the increase in value of a $100,000 investment achieving the same rate of return as Systematic's portfolios beginning on January 1, 1981, through June 30, 1992, compared to the performance of the S&P 500 and the rate of increase in the consumer price index (CPI).

I. HISTORY

Kenneth S. Hackel was born in Brooklyn, New York, in 1950. After receiving a B.B.A. in economics from the City College of New York, he obtained an M.B.A. from Baruch College and then began his career as a security analyst. At the beginning of 1983, he began Systematic's operations. Hackel is the author of many articles on investments, as well as the coauthor with New York University professor Joshua Livnat of the Business One Irwin book *Cash Flow and Securities Analysis*. He has appeared on PBS's "Wall Street Week" and regularly appears on CNN's "Money Line" and on CNBC/FNN. His comments regularly appear in leading financial periodicals such as *Business Week*.

In March 1986, Hackel enlisted the services of Jason J. Wallach, director of investment management research for E. F. Hutton & Co., Inc., who had been dealing with Systematic since its inception. Wallach is a graduate of Rutgers College, where he received a B.A. in economics.

In September 1991, Stephen D. Gresham joined Systematic as managing director-investor services. Gresham oversees all of systematic's marketing efforts. He had been associated with Systematic while holding the position of managing director-investment

EXHIBIT 12–2
Systematic Financial Management, Inc. (Mountain Chart Performance Comparison)

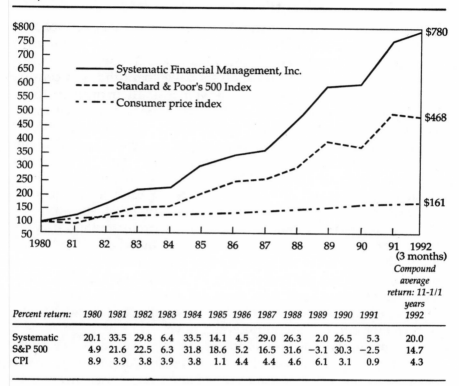

Percent return:	1980	1981	1982	1983	1984	1985	1986	1987	1988	1989	1990	1991	Compound average return: 11-1/1 years 1992
Systematic	20.1	33.5	29.8	6.4	33.5	14.1	4.5	29.0	26.3	2.0	26.5	5.3	20.0
S&P 500	4.9	21.6	22.5	6.3	31.8	18.6	5.2	16.5	31.6	−3.1	30.3	−2.5	14.7
CPI	8.9	3.9	3.8	3.9	3.8	1.1	4.4	4.4	4.6	6.1	3.1	0.9	4.3

management services with Advest, Inc. Gresham is a graduate of Brown University.

Systematic's offices are located in Fort Lee, New Jersey, just across the George Washington Bridge from Manhattan. The firm employs 21 employees, with 8 in the client relations, trading, and administrative areas. Systematic had $800 million under management as of March 1993. It strives to give its clients the highest level of service. Portfolio managers are always available to discuss Systematic's investment positions and market outlook. Moreover, it sends all clients an informative and sometimes humorous quarterly newsletter, in addition to all customary client reports.

II. STRATEGY—HOW SYSTEMATIC CONSTRUCTS A PORTFOLIO

A. How Most Analysts Select Stocks

The question that comes to mind, to which Systematic cannot offer a satisfactory answer, is "Why doesn't the investment community at large learn how to take advantage of free cash flow?" A speculative response might be that analysts have spent the past century using reported earnings and book values as their primary tools. Inertia is a sometimes insuperable force, especially in investment management firms which date back to the time of Graham & Dodd or earlier. In business newspapers on any day, countless headlines announce earnings or the lack thereof. Rarely is there an article detailing a company's cash flow—until the company is named as an acquisition target (as a result of strong cash flows) or is in jeopardy of bankruptcy (as a result of negative cash flows).

To understand Systematic's selection of investments, it is important to first understand what the firm avoids. The valuation tools which generally form the arsenal of the community of fundamental, or value-oriented, investors are (1) reported earnings, earnings forecasts, and price-earnings multiples; (2) book values and price/book value multiples; (3) asset appraisals and liquidation values; and (4) discounted cash flows.

Systematic gives no weight to the first group of tools. All public companies determine earnings using accrual accounting, which aims at providing investors with a theoretical measure of the amount by which a company's operations have increased net worth. That measure is obtained by trying to match, or report in the same period, expenses with the revenues associated with those expenses. Revenues and the associated expenses are reported during the period in which the revenues are deemed earned. Unfortunately, companies are given discretion in determining when revenues are earned. Except in a few regulated industries, such as insurance and energy, companies rarely wait to recognize revenues until cash, or other consideration, is received.

Many investment advisers espouse a low price/earnings stock selection strategy (buying the companies that offer the best bargain—i.e., the lowest stock price—given a specific amount of earnings). Hackel and his crew at Systematic reject that strategy because "more low-P/E stocks have gone bankrupt than high-P/E stocks. Since 1986, the P/E strategy has not worked for investors." Hackel continued, "Look at Unisys. The company reported record earnings and looked cheap, but it has performed poorly because it generates negative free cash flow. Another example was Integrated Resources. It was a bargain with a P/E of 7. Now it is in bankruptcy." According to Hackel, "Low P/E investing is a philosophy whose time has come and gone. With the advent of extensive computer screening, it [low P/E calculations] no longer has an edge."

But how does one spend or sell earnings? Ask the owner of the corner grocery store what matters—it is cash flow. That is what is used to distribute dividends, to pay salaries and other expenses, and to invest in the expansion of a business.

Given the substantial latitude allowed each company in selecting its method for accounting for revenues and expenses, it is almost impossible to fairly compare earnings of companies in different industries, or for that matter, different companies in the same industry. Further, changes in accounting policies often make it difficult to compare one company's earnings from year to year.

Systematic also disregards the second group of tools. Since earnings are reflected each period in an adjustment to a company's stockholder equity, book value and book value multiples pick up the static attributable to earnings distortions. More importantly, conservative accounting rules prohibit companies from reflecting the market values of appreciated assets, but require that marketable securities be valued at the lower of cost or market price.

Accurate assessments of asset values provide helpful information in determining a security's value. However, the marketability of assets other than cash and cash equivalents often fluctuates dramatically. For an example, consider the recent decline in prices for commercial real estate, the asset many analysts considered to add value above reported book values. Another example is the precipitous decline in marketability of machinery and equipment usually associated with downswings in any industry's business cycle.

To conservatively value a security, the value of illiquid assets must be discounted to reflect their illiquidity. This approach is similar to that of a commercial lender that will not advance more than a prescribed fraction of the purchase price of inventory and long-term assets. "Asset plays" often are high-risk ventures. An acquirer who is trying to garner profits by liquidating assets but is not lucky enough to properly time the market (see the discussion in the Nicholas-Applegate chapter on page 129) will be forced to accept lower-than-anticipated proceeds in order to satisfy its creditors—unless the company happens to generate free cash flow. While Systematic considers the value of assets not reflected in balance sheets, it does so in evaluating companies, not in the context of their liquidation values, but rather in defining the amount of cash that might be realized on account of those assets while the companies operate as going concerns.

Systematic agrees with the basic philosophy of traditional discounted cash-flow analysis: the value of an entity is the present value of its cash on hand and expected cash inflows minus the cash flow of its liabilities. However, unlike other analysts, Systematic does not base its analyses simply on cash flows from operations or the simplistic definition of free cash flow employed by corporate raiders during the 1980s. Those financial entrepreneurs merely added cash flows from operations and income taxes paid and then subtracted capital expenditures to determine their rather naive version of free cash flow. The use of cash flows from operations alone does not provide much guidance in that there is a strong correlation between cash flow from operations and reported earnings.

B.   How Systematic Selects Stocks—Free Cash Flow Doesn't Lie

Systematic only invests in companies with consistently positive and growing cash flows from operations. However, the real reason for investing is to receive free cash flow. Systematic determines free cash flow by adjusting reported cash flows from operations using a proprietary methodology aimed at normalizing various expenditures for fluctuations which occur throughout a business cycle. These adjustments are intended to reflect the cash used for capital expenditures necessary to support unit sales growth and eliminate the effect of "corporate fat"—excessive expenditures typically associated with business expansions and eliminated in the course of business contractions. Corporate fat may result from management's desire to provide for itself and employees with the rewards of growth, or it may be a reflection of management's inattention to expense controls. Hackel and his staff turn a company upside down searching for possible savings. Potential areas of excessive expenditures include capital expenditures, research and development, and marketing and administrative expenses. Those effects provide a degree of financial flexibility in that cash flows can be maintained during leaner (or more efficient) times through the reversal of over-expenditures.

More specifically, Systematic reduces operating cash flow by an entity's capital expenditures, less a portion of the increase in those expenditures to the extent they have increased at a rate greater than the rate of increase in cost of goods sold. The cash proceeds or cash uses for other investing activities not involving marketable securities are then added or subtracted. Systematic next adds back a portion of research and development expenses to the extent they have increased at a rate exceeding the rate of increase in cost of goods sold. Systematic then adds back a portion of the increase in selling, general, and administrative expenses to the extent they have increased at a rate exceeding the rate of sales growth. Systematic also evaluates entities' pension plans. Overfunded pension plans are viewed as a source of free cash flow, and underfunded plans are seen as users of free cash flow.

In discussing the specific definition and calculation of free cash flow, Jason Wallach commented, "There are a lot of imposter definitions utilized by investment managers. The predominant definition of *free cash flow* is profits plus depreciation, minus capital spending, minus preferred dividends." According to Hackel, that definition is wrong: "You cannot add four numbers based on accrual accounting and—poof!—it becomes free cash flow. It is not that simple."

Systematic's extensive computer facilities screen approximately 17,000 equity securities to find a few dozen which satisfy Systematic's buy criteria (see Exhibit 12-3). Those criteria relate not only to the amount of free cash flow relative to current market prices (the free cash flow yield), but also to the ability to repay debt. Off–balance sheet debt, such as operating leases, must be in-

EXHIBIT 12–3
Security Selection: Buy Criteria

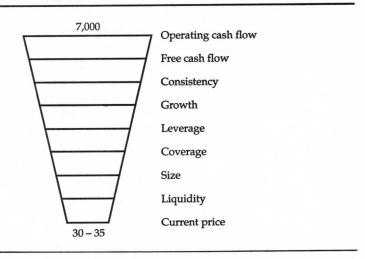

7,000	Operating cash flow
	Free cash flow
	Consistency
	Growth
	Leverage
	Coverage
	Size
	Liquidity
30 – 35	Current price

cluded in the total debt figure. On the free cash flow and debt criteria, Hackel was emphatic: "We only buy stocks that sell at less than 15 times their free cash flow, and we sell them when they rise to 20 times free cash flow. Leverage can be dangerous, if not suicidal, for a company. Total debt within companies is growing at a scary 14 percent rate, way in excess of our country's gross national product." If growth remains slow in the 1990s, which is a strong possibility, heavily leveraged companies will not have the financial flexibility to take advantage of investment opportunities, while the bankruptcy rate will remain high.

Additional criteria related to minimum market capitalization and trading volume are aimed at assuring the liquidity of Systematic's investments. Systematic wants to ensure that its portfolio managers can easily buy and sell the security without impacting the market price. Only companies that trade at least $5 million per month are considered.

Consistent free cash flow and reasonable debt servicing requirements give the companies in which Systematic invests the financial flexibility to weather industry downturns. In other words, companies with strong free cash flow do not go broke. Most of these companies already have survived the vagaries of the general economy over long periods. Hackel commented,

> All too often, money managers examine last year's cash flow only and do not analyze the consistency of the cash flow over several business cycles. You cannot extrapolate one year's free cash flow. Otherwise, you buy at the peak of cash flow and end up with a lousy investment when business conditions turn bad. It is important to analyze at least 10 years of a company's free cash flow. We do this to see how bad an entity's cash flow can get during a negative business cycle.

Systematic's portfolio managers are especially wary of companies that become big borrowers of capital during poor economic times. They seek companies that have the ability to control their cash flow swings, such as food and energy companies. For example, energy companies adjust their level of discretionary expenditures, including high exploration costs, when oil prices decline.

Systematic leaves to others the task of selecting newly issued securities, turnaround situations, or emerging growth stocks, all of which offer the opportunity for extraordinary returns for those willing to bear equally extraordinary risks. Many analysts may find Systematic's investments boring. Systematic is pleased to be bored by the consistent returns these investments have provided.

Next, Systematic screens the 7,000 companies for *growth* of cash flow. Wallach stated, "We only like to buy stocks of entities that have a positive real rate of free cash flow growth. Otherwise, you buy companies that are cannibalizing their assets to generate cash flow."

The stability of its portfolios is promoted by Systematic's practice of weighting investments equally among 30 to 35 equity securities. Systematic also manages balanced accounts comprised of specified portions of equity and fixed-income securities. Balanced accounts are suitable investments for clients who require that their portfolios regularly generate a specified level of distributable cash without the need to liquidate holdings.

Before a particular security is purchased or sold, Systematic's investment policy committee extensively reviews information from a variety of sources including, but not limited to, filings with the Securities and Exchange Commission, national and trade newspapers and periodicals and, when permitted, interviews with executive officers of the issuer of the security.

C.   When Systematic Sells a Stock

Systematic will hold an investment, often for several years, until it believes that the market price of the investment fairly reflects the issuer's free cash flow. Systematic will not buy a security unless it can do so at a price not greater than 70 percent of the security's perceived value at the date of purchase. Any adverse change in an entity's cash-flow characteristics (including changes likely to impair the ability to generate future cash flows) may result in a sale. For instance, negative operating cash flow or inconsistency in free cash flow would trigger a sale.

At times, portfolio-holding sales have occurred through no choice of Hackel and his portfolio managers. Many holdings have been subject to takeovers, meaning Systematic has been too good in its stock selection. J. P. Stevens, NCR, and Coroon & Black are just a few of the companies in the portfolio which have been taken out.

D.   Systematic Is Not a Market Timer

The securities industry is divided into two general schools of investors: technicians, who attempt to assess future investment returns by extrapolating from historical price movements, and fundamentalists, who seek to assess the true value of securities. Some analysts keep one foot in each area, both pursuing value and seeking to time the market. As stated earlier, Systematic does not engage in technical analysis or market timing.

While Systematic eschews technical analysis, it does consider fundamental macroeconomic information such as interest rates, the growth in the money supply, and the free cash-flow yield of the S&P industrials in allocating funds between equity investments and cash equivalents. Systematic's buy discipline results in weighting its portfolios heavily toward equities when the market is undervalued (free cash-flow yields are high relative to interest rates) and when there is a greater selection of securities meeting Systematic's stringent criteria. For instance, the state of the economy will impact interest rates. If interest rates rise to 10 percent, the firm's cash-flow growth rate criteria will also move up, which automatically screens out most companies, thereby reducing its portfolio stock weightings.

EXHIBIT 12–4
Systematic Financial Management, Inc. (Performance in Bull and Bear Quarters)

Return: Equity portfolios

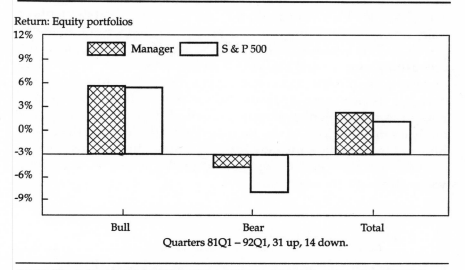

Quarters 81Q1 – 92Q1, 31 up, 14 down.

© 1992 RS&A Consulting Inc. The information presented above is based on information and data obtained from the custodian of the funds, the investment manager, or publicly available sources. It is believed to be accurate, but no representation or warranty is made as to its accuracy or completeness.

Conversely, Systematic will include a greater amount of bonds and cash equivalents in its portfolios when the market is overvalued, as determined by the relatively small number of investment candidates satisfying those criteria. Systematic's equity portfolios historically have ranged from being 65 percent to 98 percent invested in equity securities. For example, just prior to the stock market crash of 1987, only 26 stocks (and 25 to 30 percent cash) were held in client portfolios, because fewer stocks met Systematic's buy criteria. In mid-1987, the Standard & Poor's industrials sold at 28 times free cash flow, and, typically, a figure above 27 indicates a danger zone.

The accuracy of free cash-flow yields as a precursor of market moves has led Systematic to outperform the broad market in both bull and bear markets. Exhibit 12–4 shows that Systematic has outperformed the S&P 500 by an even greater margin in bear markets than in bull markets.

E. FAS No. 95 and the Awakening of the Financial Community

In November 1987 the Financial Accounting Standards Board issued FAS No. 95. It requires that businesses provide statements of cash flows, superseding the statement of changes in financial position. The issuance of FAS No. 95 signifies, at long last, the accounting authorities' realization of the importance to investors of cash flow information. Systematic believes that this focus will enhance its performance in the future as it reaps the rewards of being the preeminent cash-flow analytical firm. Hopefully, other analysts may begin to draw their attention to the cash-flow attributes of Systematic's investments. Of course, Systematic will endeavor to remain a few steps ahead of the crowd in discerning values through free cash flow.

III. SUMMARY

Systematic's free cash flow analysis has demonstrated an amazing ability to identify acquisition targets, which has been very favorable to shareholders. It also has enabled Systematic to avoid the disaster stocks resulting from overleveraging in the 1980s.

Systematic will never be a large megamanager because of its strict free cash and trading volume ($5 million in trading per month) criteria. At $1 billion under management, Hackel will stop taking new money from investors. This maximum dollar figure could be increased if the international markets continue to allow outside investors and their respective accounting systems lend themselves to free cash flow analysis.

Systematic, when compared to other free cash flow managers, is a purist. Although many managers discuss the use of free cash flow in stock selection, no one else follows Systematic's strict definition. When asked to describe a perfect free cash candidate, Hackel replied, "Currently, if we can buy companies at 10 times free cash flow with little or no debt, this means that a company can buy back all of its stock in approximately 10 years. This excess cash flow allows companies to increase capital spending, research and development, and acquisitions."

In analyzing Systematic's performance, which is exceptional, free cash flow seems to be an excellent leading indicator of positive stock price movements. For example, a company may be out of favor, but by showing improving free cash flow numbers, the stock price should awaken. Moreover, free cash flow analysis is especially helpful in down stock markets. Over the past 11 years, the S&P 500 has suffered down quarters on 14 occasions. Systematic has outperformed the S&P 500 in 12 of these 14 quarters and, to date, *has never had a down year*.

Down markets are the nemesis of the average investor because of the temptation to pull the plug. Upon receipt of the monthly/quarterly statement reflecting the paper loss when utilizing the services of Systematic, you are less likely to cash out your portfolio during a market downturn because the financial pain tends to be minimized. For example, Systematic's portfolio had recovered fully by March 1988 following the late October 1987 stock market crash. In contrast, it took the S&P 500 over one and a half years to fully recover to the precrash level. According to The Mobius Group, an independent investment management consultant, Systematic has captured about 98 percent of the market's upside, while removing 40 percent of the market's downside.

Systematic underperforms the market when the economy swings from recession to expansion, when the investing public is solely invested in turnaround companies. Predictable free cash flow companies like the Bic Corporation, a stock which more than doubled before it was sold by Systematic, are boring to managers who are looking to quadruple their money over the next two quarters.

Systematic has rejected several offers to sell its research or manage money for other investment houses. Instead, the firm prefers to work with clients who have a long-term time horizon, where portfolios are given enough time and slack to work out. Systematic turns away the fast money crowd, telling prospective clients it wants at least five years to manage the funds.

Systematic believes the market is involved in a significant rotation away from the large-capitalization, classic growth stocks that have fueled the last market upswing. Simply, Hackel and his portfolio managers believe the easy money stocks (Coca-Cola) have run out of steam. According to Systematic, with the bull market 10 years old as of August 1992, the easy money in the market has been made. In that 10-year period, virtually every disciplined style has been profitable, including those encompassing small, large, growth, and value stocks. What investment strategies will work going forward? Not surprisingly, Systematic believes that the less familiar companies such as Hillenbrand Industries, Inc. (maker of burial caskets) and Lance, Inc. (cookie and cracker company) will begin to outperform the last decade's growth stocks, Coca-Cola and Merck. Why? Instead of trading at 40 times free cash flow like Coke and Merck, Hillenbrand and Lance will trade for 12 to 15 times free cash flow. Today, Systematic is buying companies selling at 50 to 65 percent (12 to 15 times) of the free cash flow multiple of the market (23 times). Many of today's growth stocks have negative free cash flow which Systematic believes will ultimately be reflected in their respective stock prices. With U.S. economic growth remaining below normal, growth stocks could lose much of their relative appeal. As stated earlier, Systematic prefers the unglamourous, middle-sized companies. Currently, the average Systematic portfolio holding has a market capitalization of about $1.5 billion, compared to the Dow Jones 30 average of $22 billion.

Systematic portfolio managers are not disheartened by all the news surrounding the major unwinding of debt on America. Yes, these restructurings and reorganizations have a human toll (layoffs, forced retirement, plant closings, and so on), but Systematic believes these restructurings are long overdue. Cost-cutting and reorganization bodes well for increasing cash flows within companies. Companies that have demonstrated free cash flow and low debt levels have the flexibility to get a head start in the economy. But even if the country doesn't get the recovery expected, free cash flow/low debt companies will be survivors. Systematic does not feel that the market will become overvalued until it reaches a multiple of 27 to 28 times free cash flow, the peaks of the past.

In spite of the spate of bad news surrounding our economy, Systematic is very bullish on America. Systematic believes that the United States is the best-performing industrialized economy. When compared to Japan and Germany, the Americans are the low-cost producer in 7 of the 11 primary manufacturing industries.

In summary, portfolio management is both an art and a science. Systematic's approach is heavily steeped in science. Cash-flow analysis seems so easy at its face value as being analogous to a family's discretionary spending income. Systematic's style seems to be especially appropriate for the decade of the 1990s, where there is a renewed focus on personal, government, and corporate debt reduction. Systematic's disciplined style has a natural attraction to our basic, practical business instincts. Every day we see companies, government, and individuals whose problems are either created or exacerbated by excessive debt. For these reasons, Systematic is appropriate for investors seeking a no-nonsense, conservative equity style.

As you can see, determining true free cash flow entails a substantial amount of financial investigation. By focusing on low or nonexistent debt and the need for excess free cash flow, Systematic seems to be one step ahead of the crowd—not bad for a strategy considered to be bland, boring, and reserved for those nerdy accounting types. It may be boring—but it works!

Chapter Thirteen

Summary
What We Can Learn from These Pros

Where does one begin to summarize a year's worth of interviews with 10 of the top-ranked investment advisers, who collectively manage over $25 billion? Below, hundreds of random thoughts are summarized and organized into a few key points.

I. STICK TO YOUR GUNS THROUGH THICK AND THIN

Several of the managers, without prodding, used the sport of boxing to describe not only what they do but how they manage their lives. This same theme came up time and time again and goes something like this:

> In boxing, you have to know when to take the offensive, when to retreat to a defensive position, how to dodge the big hits and, *most importantly*, how to get off the canvas when you have taken what looks and feels like a knockdown blow to your head. You've taken a direct hit to the face (meaning you are losing both clientele and their money because your strategy is not working), and the referee is beginning the countdown (many of your clients have lost confidence in you and your abilities), but at the nine count, when everyone believes you are finished, you somehow pull yourself off the canvas, stand up to your opponent and finish the round, severely wounded, but still fighting!

Each of the managers has, at one time, taken a terrible beating in the stock and bond markets. They have all lost, not only money, but clientele. Yet they did not quit. Kenneth Fisher, in discussing this common characteristic among top managers, stated,

Most young investment advisers, especially those who have attended America's most prestigious schools, expect to have a shot at being the next Peter Lynch. Unfortunately, the real world doesn't work that way. After some initial success, they take their first big blow [loss] and that is it. They are finished. Only those with a rough-and-tumble attitude survive. This is a dirty, tough business, and most people cannot take the constant heat and disappointments.

Roger Engemann commented further, "I do not believe any of the 10 managers interviewed in this book are any smarter than a lot of investment advisers, but they do have a gumption level not seen in most humans."

Just as you should be wary (and should consider firing!) an investment adviser who abandons his style during periods when his style is out of sync with the overall market, never bail out of an investment account just because you're in the middle of a bear market. It is unreasonable to expect an equity manager to make a bundle of money when the markets are lousy. Instead, bear markets or down quarters are a great time to evaluate the behavior of your manager and, if you like what you see, place additional funds with him.

Investment styles, over the short-term market cycles, ebb and flow. One quarter, your adviser's style is hot and the next, cold as a stone. You cannot time when your adviser's style is going to be in or out of favor; therefore, don't even attempt it. Rather, focus on the long term.

II.   THERE ARE NO MAGIC FORMULAS— EXPECT TO BUILD WEALTH SLOWLY

Although the equity and bond markets have proven to be the best places to build long-term wealth, they do not lend themselves to foolproof investment strategies, systems, or black box models. None of the managers interviewed in this book have developed "slam-dunk" money-making strategies we so often hear about in radio and TV advertising or the financial press. Instead, they have committed, as should all of us, to an investment philosophy and strategy which makes sense to them.

III.   TRUST YOUR ADVISERS— LET THEM DO THEIR THING

You have accurately defined your investment risk profile and comfort zone and have searched for, reviewed, and selected a money manager that matches your outlook and investment personality. Now comes the hard part. Let the investment adviser do his thing! Do not meddle. Give your manager enough rope to implement his style.

IV.   BEFORE INVESTING, UNDERSTAND THE RISK YOU ARE FACING

"Security is mostly a superstition. It does not exist in nature. Life is either a daring adventure or nothing."

Helen Keller, *The Open Door*

Investors face a variety of risks—market, company, volatility, inflation, and deflation. For most investors, something more elementary must be addressed before investing *one dime:* Should your principal be at risk? Should you be in the market at all? The most difficult, yet most important part of the manager selection process has little to do with the adviser himself—rather it centers on developing a clear comfort zone of risk. If the answer is yes to market participation, then you should expect market volatility and be prepared for it.

V.   PREDICTING THE MARKET'S DIRECTION—FORGET SHORT-TERM MOVES, FOCUS ON EXTREMES

The interviewed managers denounce anyone's ability to predict the exact bottom or top in individual stocks/bonds or the markets. Rather, they look for extreme under- and overvaluations. During extreme overvaluations, they will lighten up their stock portfolio and/or shift to less volatile equities and bonds. Conversely, during extreme undervaluations, they will take a more aggressive stance. Most felt that it is a waste of time trying to predict the next short-term market move. No one, not even the savvy advisers reviewed in this book, have any idea where the market is going over the next three to six months. Instead, most focus on the next 3 to 10 years and stock and bond selection, ignoring all the noise—financial news including daily facts and figures.

VI.   BEWARE OF THE "GEORGE STEINBRENNER SYNDROME"

Just as the contrarian investment approach to the market is preferred, the same principle applies to selecting a money manager. A sure way to underperform the market is to consistently invest with last year's winners. How many times do you see last year's top mutual fund heading the list two years later? Very seldom! Put simply, past performance has little predictive ability for future performance. One of the risks of this book is to assume that the 10 managers highlighted in this book will continue to outperform the markets and their peers. You need to be warned of falling into the often-cited "George Steinbrenner Syndrome" (coined from a *Financial Analysts Journal* article by Michael L. Troutman), which is to hire the managers (or top baseball players) with the best recent performance, only to find they fail to live up to the expectations or their pay. Rather, a client and financial adviser must analyze the performance for *consistency* over 5- to 10-year periods, especially during the low periods, not whether they led the league in hitting last year. In fact, the most prudent approach is to select a manager who has an excellent track record and proven style but who has underperformed because his style is not in vogue.

VII.   DECIDE IF YOU ARE ABSOLUTE OR RELATIVE PERFORMANCE DRIVEN

It is unfair to tell your money manager that you cannot live with a negative return in any given year *but* he must beat the S&P 500 during the good years. Mission impossible—you cannot have it

EXHIBIT 13–1
The Process

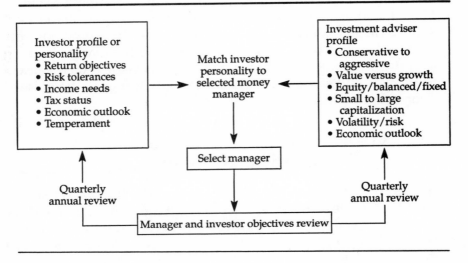

both ways. Either you are willing to underperform the markets during up phases but outperform during the bear market periods, or you tell him you are interested in excellent relative performance, which means you should expect both greater potential returns and greater volatility.

VIII.   SELECT A STYLE THAT FITS YOU— 10 WAYS TO SKIN A CAT

Each of the managers explained the importance of not accepting client capital that does not fit their firm's specific investment philosophy and strategy. As Roger Engemann stated, "There are some clients you should just pass on. Anytime we are presented a potential client whose objectives don't match ours, the return and risk expectations are unreasonable, or he/she exhibits high emotional characteristics, we suggest they select another manager. Otherwise, these clients will make our already difficult job impossible."

IX. FINAL COMMENTS

The entire investment management process is graphically depicted for you in Exhibit 13–1. Additionally, a matrix guide briefly describing each of the 10 managers is presented in Exhibit 13–2. This guide should help you with the comparison of different managers and styles.

Upon the completion of the manager interviews and rough draft of this text, a client, after hearing of my work, called me to ask one simple question—"So, Doug, which manager is the best?" I paused, thought about the question and then mumbled something like, "Oh, I don't know, which is a better fruit—an apple or an orange?" I continued, "Better yet, who was the best athlete to ever play a specific sport—Michael Jordan, Carl Lewis, Magic Johnson, Joe Montana, Mohammed Ali, or Arnold Palmer?"

Yes, I do have some preferences, but that is not because one manager is "better" than the rest. Rather, my preferences stem directly from my investment personality. Each investor has a unique investment personality, which covers risk and volatility tolerances, return objectives, income needs, economic opinions, and views of the world. Some of us are bargain shoppers—we cannot stand to pay full price for anything. We only want what we perceive as good buys, whether they are in investments or daily purchases. Others want only the best companies in America today. If it is going out to dinner, going on vacation, or buying 100 shares of Coca-Cola, we only want what is characterized and recognized as the best. Thus, it is critical that a chemistry exists between you and your selected manager. It may be difficult to explain, but you know when you have it.

It is important that you do not allow anyone but yourself to define your investment personality. Many investors, by concentrating solely on rate-of-return data, neglect the most important facet of selecting a money manager: Does the investment manager's style fit my investment personality? As discussed earlier, using the racetrack method for picking money managers (where you place all your bets on the winner of the last race) can be a prescription for poor investment results.

Yes, the people interviewed are some of the most thoughtful and insightful investment managers in America today. And yes,

EXHIBIT 13–2
Manager Grid

Highlighted Managers	Investment Style
Avatar Associates	Active asset allocation—stocks, bonds, and cash
Brandes Investment Partners, Inc.	Global/international—strict Graham & Dodd style
Roger Engemann & Associates	Classic growth—seeks companies exhibiting consistent earnings growth
Fisher Investments	Value—low price/sales ratio, small capitalization
Fox Asset Management	Value—low P/E ratio and debt, high dividends and cash flow
Harris Bretall Sullivan & Smith Inc.	Growth—medium to large capitalization, dividend discount model, earnings momentum, price momentum
Nicholas-Applegate Capital Management	Growth (worldwide)—small to medium capitalization, relative strength/price momentum
Regent Investor Services	Sector rotator—growth/value rotation analysis of economic, political, and social trends
Rittenhouse Financial Services	Growth—classic with cyclical, blue chip, large capitalization
Systematic Financial Management, Inc.	Value—free cash analysis, low debt

their track records are outstanding within their respective styles, in the top 10 percent. But I want to make it clear that the stock and bond markets are fickle and unpredictable. I believe Roger Engemann put it accurately: "The market is like a train sitting on the tracks. You can see the direction it's heading, but you cannot dictate the time of departure. Those investors who put the market on a timetable not only become frustrated but end up making foolish moves. Instead, get on the train, sit back, and enjoy the scenery." Words of wisdom we all should adhere to.

Appendixes

Investor Profile Questionnaire

1. What is your attitude toward the U.S. economy over the next three to five years?

   A. Very negative.

   B. Somewhat negative.

   C. Neutral.

   D. Somewhat positive.

   E. Very positive.

2. The perception of investment risk may differ from investor to investor. Please indicate the description of risk below that most closely describes your views.

   A. Chance of significant loss in an overall portfolio.

   B. Gradual erosion of the portfolio.

   C. Significant portfolio fluctuations despite their being in line with the overall market.

   D. Erosion of purchasing power/not keeping pace with inflation.

   E. Overexposure to equities in the overall portfolio.

3. How would you expect your portfolio to be managed?

   A. Maximum growth—emphasize appreciation over income. Seeks equities where higher risks are taken in search of higher rewards over the long term. Near-term price volatility is possible.

   B. Long-term growth—emphasize appreciation with some consideration for income. Seeks equities of well-established companies, diversified for growth and/or income. Less volatility than maximum growth category is expected.

C. Growth plus fixed income—emphasize appreciation and current income. Seeks a portfolio balanced between stocks, bonds, and cash. Target consistent results with moderate price volatility.

D. Income—seeks income and preservation of capital employing bonds, convertibles, and/or cash equivalents.

4. Rank from 1–4 the investment objectives below in order of importance to you in terms of your attitude toward your portfolio (1 being most important and 4 being least important).

_____ Preservation of capital—over the investment time horizon, capital gains are to be protected and an average rate of return maintained.

_____ Preservation of purchasing power—equal or exceed rate of inflation over the investment time horizon.

_____ Growth of capital—obtain above-average total return.

_____ Aggressive growth of capital—achieve maximum total return even though it may entail taking substantial risk.

5. The overall investment objective of this portfolio over a market cycle is to:

A. Avoid long-term erosion of capital (preservation of capital).

B. At least keep pace if not exceed the inflation rate (preservation of purchasing power).

C. Achieve a positive rate of return on capital.

D. Perform favorably relative to known market indices (S&P 500, etc.).

E. Exceed returns available from risk-free investments (T-bills) while conforming to major market movements.

F. Produce a steady income stream which equals or exceeds those available from money market instruments (not available for equity portfolios).

6. Do you require current income?
   A. Require current income flow (not available for equity portfolios).
   B. Current dividends and/or interest is considered a significant component of total return, but current income is not required.
   C. Current income is not required.
7. Dividend yield is one guide to the type of stocks that might be emphasized in a portfolio. Generally, the higher the anticipated capital appreciation or growth of a stock, the smaller its dividend yield. Select the statement consistent with your investment philosophy.
   A. Growth is more important than dividend yield.
   B. Stocks should be diversified across growth and yield-oriented securities.
   C. Stocks paying high dividends should be emphasized.
8. How would you like to have your portfolio managed?
   A. With very little risk in order to obtain stable returns.
   B. With some risk in order to receive average returns.
   C. With the expectation of receiving better-than-average returns while taking the chance of losing part of your money.
   D. With the opportunity to receive maximum returns while taking the chance of losing a substantial portion of your money.
9. If your investment should decline by 20 percent of its value in one month, assuming that none of the fundamentals have changed, do you:
   A. Hold it and wait for it to go back up?
   B. Sell it?
   C. Buy more because it looks even more attractive?
10. Investment risk can be measured by the degree of volatility of a portfolio's market value from period to period. Which statement best describes your risk tolerance? Assume that returns are relative to the amount of risk taken.
    A. Willing to accept a high degree of fluctuation in market value with a possibility of more than one year of negative absolute returns over a market cycle, for the potential of higher returns.

    B. Willing to accept market value fluctuations with a possibility of two or three quarters of negative absolute returns through difficult phases in a market cycle.

    C. Willing to accept a modest degree of market value fluctuation where infrequent, very moderate losses occur in general market movements for the potential of consistent, average returns.

11. Please circle the letter of the portfolio whose five-year investment average is most in keeping with your own preference and expectations.

Year 1	Year 2	Year 3	Year 4	Year 5	5 Year Average
A. + 8%	+5%	+ 8%	+ 7%	+ 6%	+ 7%
B. +27%	−4%	+22%	+18%	− 5%	+11%
C. +37%	−9%	+39%	+32%	−10%	+16%

12. What do you anticipate that the rate of inflation will be over the next 10 years?

    A. Less than 2%.

    B. 2–4%.

    C. 4–5%.

    D. 5–7%.

    E. Above 7%.

13. If risk is measured on a scale of 1–10, 1 being the most conservative and 10 being the most aggressive, where on this scale would you feel *most comfortable?* (Circle one number.)

    more conservative 1 2 3 4 5 6 7 8 9 10 more aggressive

14. Where on the scale is the *highest* or *maximum* level of risk that you are willing to assume? The answer indicated should be at least as high as your answer to Question 13. (Circle one number.)

    less risk 1 2 3 4 5 6 7 8 9 10 more risk

15. How long are you willing to wait for the results you expect in this program?

    A. Less than three years.

    B. Three to five years.

C. Five to 10 years.

D. More than 10 years.

16. What average maturity in your bond portfolio do you feel is appropriate for this account?

   A. Under five years (short term).

   B. Five to 10 years (intermediate).

   C. Eleven or more years (long term).

   D. Maturity structure is decision of money manager.

17. Will you require income from the account?

   ____ Yes   Monthly $ _____ Quarterly $ _____

   ____ No

   ____ Other $ _____ (list amount and frequency)

18. Which type of account would you prefer? Please see account descriptions.

Equity-Oriented Accounts	*Balanced Accounts*
____ Growth	____ Balanced
____ Equity income	____ Flexible balanced/asset allocation
____ Aggressive growth	____ Fixed income
____ Value style (check one)	____ International/global
____ Large company	
____ Medium company	
____ Small company	

Appendix B

Sample Investment Policy Statement

I. STATEMENT OF PURPOSE

The purpose of this statement is to establish a clear understanding between _____ (hereinafter referred to as "the Client") and the Asset Management firm regarding investment objectives, goals, and guidelines for "The Fund." It is intended to provide meaningful guidance in the management of Fund assets and not be overly restrictive given the changing economic, business, and investment market conditions. The determination of investment goals and objectives is based solely on the responses provided by the _____ client profile and questionnaire.

This document should be reviewed on a periodic basis by the Client, and any modifications should be discussed with the _____ Financial Adviser.

This Fund was established to set aside monies for investment purposes.

It is intended that approximately $100,000 will be placed with an independent Asset Management firm within the _____ program for portfolio management purposes.

II. INVESTMENT OBJECTIVES

The Fund is an equity-oriented portfolio comprised of common stock, convertibles, and cash equivalent securities and is intended to be structured more aggressively than balanced portfolios.

In accordance with investment objectives stated below, assets in the Fund should be managed in a moderately conservative manner. In this context, conservative relates to such issues as expected long-term rates of return and return volatility, investment vehicles, diversification among economic and industry sectors, and individual securities.

Within this framework, the primary investment objective is:

Growth of Capital—The asset value of the Plan, exclusive of contributions or withdrawals, should grow in the long run and earn a rate of return in excess of an equity market index while incurring less risk than such index.

The secondary but also important investment objective of the Fund:

Preservation of Purchasing Power—Asset growth, exclusive of contributions and withdrawals, should exceed the rate of inflation in order to preserve the purchasing power of participants' assets.

III. INVESTMENT GOALS

Based on the investment objectives stated above, the primary goal of the Fund is:

In the long term, to equal or exceed the return of the Standard and Poor's 500 stock index (S&P 500).

A secondary goal is:

To equal or exceed the inflation rate (as measured by the Consumer Price Index or CPI) on an annualized basis.

These investment goals are expected to be achieved over less than three years.

IV. INVESTMENT GUIDELINES

General:

Investments are to be made consistent with the safeguards and diversity to which a prudent investor would adhere.

Subject to the limitations stated herein, the Asset Manager is given full investment discretion consistent with the investment objectives and guidelines of this Fund. The Asset Manager shall have full discretion regarding the purchase and sale of individual securities and the selection between equity securities and cash equivalents in order to assure full flexibility in the management of the Fund.

Neither the Asset Management firm nor ⎯⎯⎯⎯ will take any tax-related issues into consideration in the management of the assets within the ⎯⎯⎯⎯ program. The client should contact his or her own tax professional on tax issues.

Realization of capital gains and losses should be viewed solely in terms of investment merits.

All assets selected for the portfolio must have a readily available market value and be marketable.

Equity Investments:

The Fund may consist of common stocks and convertible preferred stocks, convertible fixed-income securities, and cash reserves.

It should be well-diversified to avoid undue exposure to any single economic sector, industry group, or individual security.

Common stocks and convertible preferred stocks should be of good quality and listed on either the New York Stock Exchange or American Stock Exchange or traded in the over-the-counter market with the requirement that such stocks have adequate market liquidity relative to the size of the investment.

Short-Term Investments:

Short-term investments shall consist of individual fixed-income securities such as certificates of deposit, commercial paper, U.S. Treasury bills, and other similar instruments with less than one year to maturity and/or money market funds.

V.   INVESTMENT PERFORMANCE REVIEW

The Asset Manager's performance results will be measured on a quarterly basis ⎯⎯⎯⎯. Total Fund performance will be measured against commonly accepted market comparisons.

Consideration shall be given to the extent to which the investment results are consistent with the investment objectives and goals as set forth in the Statement.

VI. COMMUNICATIONS

Communications with the Client:

Written confirmation on every transaction.

Monthly statements summarizing the valuation of the fund and displaying a detailed listing of transactions.

Provide quarterly market overview which will serve as a review of the previous quarter and an outlook on the upcoming quarter.

Quarterly performance reviews will be provided by your _____ Financial Adviser which will show the fund results.

Client Communications:

On a timely basis, provide the Asset Manager through the _____ Financial Adviser with any change in your circumstances which might affect the investment of your assets.

VII. SUMMARY

All investments are to be made in a prudent manner.

It is expected that the Asset Manager will manage the assets so that the results will meet the objectives and goals as set forth in this Statement.

This Statement is intended to be used as a guideline rather than a rigid statement of policy from which there can be no deviation. However, it is anticipated that any important deviations, and the reasons therefore, will be brought to the attention of _____ and the Client on a timely basis.

Appendix C

Quarterly Performance Tools/Charts

I. QUARTERLY PERFORMANCE BAR CHART (EXHIBIT C–1)

This chart measures whether and how much your manager was up and down, quarter by quarter. It treats each quarter separately; cumulative performance is not included. By reviewing this bar chart over several years, you can get an eyeball view of the degree of volatility. More specifically, during the bad market periods, how much of a drawdown/decline has the manager experienced? Many times the Standard & Poor's 500 record is included on this bar chart to assist you in the comparison. When added, this gives a graphic depiction of the value the manager added to the portfolio.

II. ACCUMULATED VALUE CHART (EXHIBIT C–2)

The second chart reports the accumulated performance versus some capital market index like the S&P 500. This gives the investor a comparison with which to match his performance over a full market cycle.

III. SCATTERGRAM CHART (EXHIBIT C–3)

The third chart measures *both* performance and volatility against a capital market index known in the industry as the scattergram. The scattergram was reviewed in the introduction to this book. Taken alone, this chart does not measure the amount of risk taken by the manager—only the volatility. To accurately measure risk undertaken by a specific manager, you must analyze the scattergram in combination with the bar and accumulated value chart.

EXHIBIT C–1
Example Investment Advisers (Risk Evaluator Rolling 4 Quarters—2, 1992)

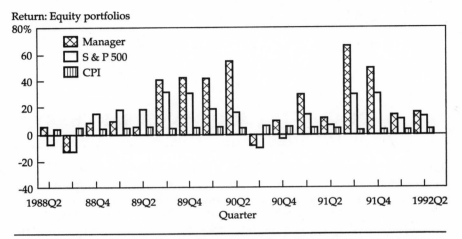

Return: Equity portfolios

EXHIBIT C–2
Example Investment Advisers (Performance Review)

Return: Equity portfolios

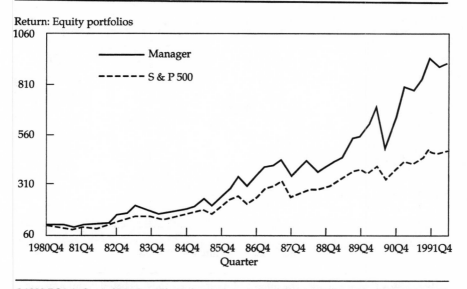

©1992 RS&A Consulting Inc. The information presented above is based on information and data obtained from the custodian of the funds, the investment manager, or publicly available sources. It is believed to be accurate, but no representation or warranty is made as to its accuracy or completeness.

EXHIBIT C–3
Example Investment Advisers (Return versus Volatility)

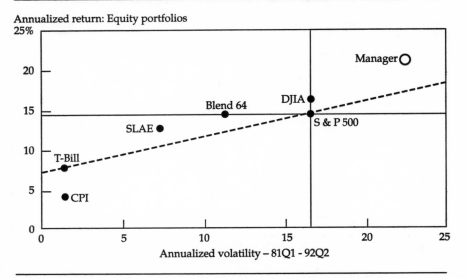

Annualized return: Equity portfolios

©1992 RS&A Consulting Inc. The information presented above is based on information and data obtained from the custodian of the funds, the investment manager, or publicly available sources. It is believed to be accurate, but no representation or warranty is made as to its accuracy or completeness.

EXHIBIT C–4
Example Investment Advisers *(Performance In Bull and Bear Quarters)*

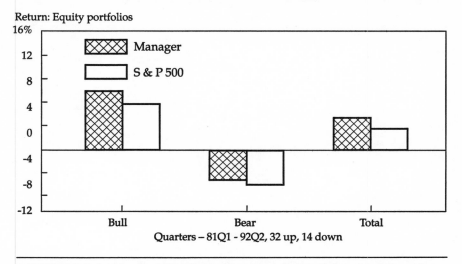

Return: Equity portfolios

Quarters – 81Q1 - 92Q2, 32 up, 14 down

©1992 RS&A Consulting Inc. The information presented above is based on information and data obtained from the custodian of the funds, the investment manager, or publicly available sources. It is believed to be accurate, but no representation or warranty is made as to its accuracy or completeness.

IV.   BULL AND BEAR MARKET CHART (EXHIBIT C–4)

This chart compares the manager's performance under both good and bad market conditions. This allows you to measure the amount of pain inflicted during the customary bear markets. Additionally, you can review how well the manager has performed during positive market periods.

Index